embrace yourself

TARYN BRUMFITT is an internationally recognised keynote speaker and the fiercely passionate thought leader behind the Body Image Movement.

Bestselling author and director of the inspiring social-change documentary *Embrace*, Taryn's global crusade to end the body dissatisfaction epidemic has seen her recognised by the United Nations Women, Amy Poehler's Smart Girls and the Geena Davis Institute.

Whether motivating the next generation at Google HQ or inspiring crowds on the international speakers circuit, Taryn's determination to shift the way people think about themself and their body has been praised as being 'good for the world'. Named alongside Beyonce and Emma Watson in *Brigitte* magazine's 'Woman of the Year', Taryn's positively infectious voice and powerful message have reached over 200 million people.

Taryn lives in Adelaide, Australia with her husband, Mathew, three children, one dog, one turtle and ten fish.

embrace yourself

TARYN BRUMFITT

PENGUIN LIFE

AN IMPRINT OF

PENGUIN BOOKS

TO THE THREE MOST
INFLUENTIAL 'M'S IN MY LIFE

Mikaela, Mum & Madonna.

THANKS FOR A LIFETIME OF INSPIRATION.

DARLING GIRL, DON'T WASTE A SINGLE DAY
OF YOUR LIFE BEING AT WAR WITH YOUR BODY.

Just Embrace it.

PENGUIN LIFE AUSTRALIA

UK | USA | Canada | Ireland | Australia
India | New Zealand | South Africa | China

Penguin Books is part of the Penguin Random House group of companies
whose addresses can be found at global.penguinrandomhouse.com.

First published by Penguin Random House Australia Pty Ltd, 2018

Cover and text design by Adam Laszczuk © Penguin Random House Australia Pty Ltd
Photography by Meg Hansen Photography
Photographs on pages 160 and 183 by Katherine Shultz Photography
Additional photography by Prue Langhans, Kate Ellis, Karen Lynch, Benjamin Liew and Andre Agnew
Printed and bound in China by RR Donnelley Asia Printing Solutions Ltd

 A catalogue record for this
book is available from the
National Library of Australia

ISBN 978 0 14378 705 1

penguin.com.au

The information contained in this book is of a general nature only. If you wish to make use of any health and
lifestyle information in this book relating to your health and lifestyle, you should first consider its appropriateness
to your situation, including consulting a medical professional.

Foreword

I FIRST WATCHED *EMBRACE* ON A FLIGHT from Australia to Los Angeles and was profoundly affected by what I saw. I was on my way to attend the 2017 Academy Awards. I had just birthed my second child, had not yet shed the baby weight and was days away from walking the biggest red carpet of my career. I felt I was under the watchful eye of Hollywood – an industry that is rife with both scrutiny and self-criticism – but watching *Embrace* carried me through those anxiety-ridden days and the weeks that followed.

The media would have us believe we need to reach a standard that is simply not realistic. Making people feel inadequate is a very profitable business! I have been photoshopped and airbrushed a thousand times over, which in the past has led to a private struggle in separating who I *am* from the way I *look*. I personally know so many women who suffer through this same battle, but watching *Embrace* reminded me that the issue is much bigger than many of us realise. We are in the midst of a heartbreaking epidemic; relentless negativity and self-loathing has become a global issue.

Embrace reinvigorated my passion for raising awareness of this toxic judgement that we project onto ourselves and each other. We must redefine and rewrite the ideals of beauty. We must not only strive to empower women to Embrace, but look to overhaul the current perception of beauty that is driven by the media and wider society. We are each whole, unique, healthy and capable just *as we are*, and it needs to be celebrated so! Let us focus on our *achievements, our dreams, our ways of being and our connections* in life rather than how we look or don't look.

I was so taken with Taryn, and I wholeheartedly believe in the importance of her mission. Embracing yourself can help you to harness the power of positive body language and prioritise mental health before beauty. Only through dedicated self-work was I able to find acceptance of my body and cultivate self-love. I support every woman in finding the courage to do this work and I know that the motivation offered by Taryn and her Body Image Movement will set you on the right path.

Taryn is warm, joyous and dedicated. She is pioneering this profound and essential movement in an exciting time of change. My hope for every person who reads this book is that they are not only inspired to embrace their own body, but that they are swept up in this powerful time and choose to take part in a society that values and celebrates people for who they are. With this mindset, it is possible that the children of our future will grow to value mental, emotional, physical wellbeing and wholeness as having the utmost importance.

My belief is that self-deprecation manifests itself out of something deeper. Perhaps on your Embrace journey there will be some confronting and uncomfortable emotions. I encourage you to dig deep, dive into those feelings and explore all that comes up. It will serve you well and bring you closer to yourself. As my favourite Rumi quote so divinely puts it, 'Don't turn away. Keep your gaze upon the bandaged place. That's where the light enters you.'

Be kind to yourself, surround yourself with a tribe of strong, warm-hearted souls and allow yourself to be whole. Free yourself from the tiring committee in your head and remind yourself to celebrate your body for all the beautiful things it can do. You are worthy of love and you can look to Taryn's words to help lift the burden of self-doubt that rests so heavily on your shoulders. This book is a gift to all women; let it be your bible.

Teresa Palmer

I'm A HIGH-SCHOOL DROPOUT. I was a rebellious teenager who got tattoos when she was fifteen and ran away from home when she was sixteen. English was my worst subject, and under no authority do I have what it takes to be an author. But I *do* have something to say.

When I speak to audiences, and share my stories and the stories of others, people's lives change. I say this with a balance of humility and fist pumps, as I'm as surprised as the next person that I can stand on a stage and impact someone's life in such a profound way.

These days, it comes quite naturally to present in front of thousands of people. Don't get me wrong, I still do a dozen nervous wees before getting on stage, complete with clammy hands and quivering voice, but rather than remain paralysed by the fear of public speaking, I now choose to dance with those nervous emotions.

A good friend gave me some advice a few years ago when I showed him my trembling hands just before going on stage to speak to 600 people.

'Look at my hands,' I said to him.

He replied, 'Taryn, when you speak it's not about *you*, it's about *them*.' Pointing to the audience, he made me realise that when you have something to say – something important to say like I do – you need to do everything within your power to go ahead and say it.

But writing a book is different to being onstage. In a book, I can't hand-flap about, raise my voice or perform pelvic thrusts to get my point across. You can't see my tears, and I can't see yours. Writing makes me feel vulnerable, and the words you are going to read in this book are going to make you feel vulnerable too. I guess we're in this together.

Speaking of vulnerability, I know that's probably how you feel as you read this. Chances are, you picked up this book because you're feeling bad about your body. This might be the first time all week you've allowed yourself to take down the mask you wear every day providing the illusion that everything's 'okay'. But it's not. I *know* it's not. Not loving your body feels like absolute crap!

I speak from experience when I say this to you. I know how exhausting it feels to spend your entire life trying to lose those last five kilos, or be consumed by the worry that summer is just around the corner and you're not adequately prepared to strut your stuff in a bikini (because we all know summer bodies are made in winter, right? More on this tripe later!).

After months of torturing my body (think weighing food, weighing myself and trying to pretend that eating food out of a plastic container was somehow fun) I realised standing there on stage in my 'perfect bikini body' that, for me, having the 'ideal' body took too much time, sacrifice and energy. For me, continuing to have my 'stage body' would require a lifetime of obsession and probably arguments with my husband, Mat. (I was very moody when I was on the bikini-body-obsession road.)

After three pregnancies in three and a half years, I felt like my body was broken. You could pick up my breasts like they were dirty tissues as they were so 'tired' after feeding 4500 meals to my children (a fact that I show off and tell as many people as I can these days!). My stomach was a jelly-belly mess covered in stretch marks. My thighs were chunky, and my arms (you know the flappy bit underneath, aka tuckshop arms) would continue to wobble well after I'd finished waving. My body was gross. Ugly. Disgusting. I hated it.

When I learnt to love my body, after hating it for most of my life, it felt like winning the golden ticket. It felt like I'd been given entry into the greatest place on earth, a place where life is magical and full of possibility. A place where you can just *be*, rather than be filled with fear that you – and your body – are not enough. That place, or state of being, is what I like to call 'embrace'.

When I posted my non-traditional 'before' and 'after' photos on social media, never in my wildest dreams did I imagine they would have the impact that they did and encourage a community of like-minded women around the world to embrace. I imagined a comment or two from my mates, of course, because hey, it's not often your friend perches her naked self on a stool to prove it's possible to love a version of yourself that's not stereotypically 'perfect'. But the magnitude of the response worldwide was mind-blowing.

It's almost laughable to think how much that photograph rocked the brains of those in the media at the time. It was headline news in almost every country of the world, and as if that wasn't enough, it made its way up into space like Buzz Aldrin! (Well, sort of.) When it was going viral, a friend of mine got off a plane and rang me immediately to say, 'You made the in-flight news!' And all because a woman loved her body?

Stop the press!

A WOMAN LOVES
HER 'IMPERFECT' BODY!

I spent the best part of a year being interviewed about that photo. Even today, years later, I'm still talking about it! We are so conditioned to think that a person losing weight will lead to a feeling of happily ever after that people simply can't wrap their heads around the fact that it simply wasn't the case for me.

While it's mostly YOU who drives me to action every day, it was the frustration I felt when doing hundreds (if not thousands) of media interviews in the beginning that drove me to finding bigger platforms – on my own terms – on which to tell my story. I discovered that the media was a great way to share a very small message, but it's impossible to change the world through tiny snippets of airtime.

Television interviews are only four minutes long, and all you need is a breaking story about a cat skateboarding through the main street of Austin, Texas, to push your story to the scrap pile. Newspapers or magazines don't promise much more success, with your words at the

hands of editors. That's why I'm so grateful for the opportunity that social media affords me, and of course, writing books like this. I can share my words, my stories – everything I want to – without being censored.

Having a golden ticket is great, but what's the point of having a yearly ticket to the greatest fun park on earth when there are not enough people for you to share it with? That's why, despite my self-doubt that I am entitled to be an author, I decided to write this book. I think of it as a baton, if you will, that I'm passing to you so that you can join me in embracing yourself too. I want you to love yourself the way that I love myself. Intensely, and with the kind of love that fills you with so much energy and joy it should probably come with a warning!

7

I was recently asked in a Facebook Live chat whether or not I have days when I feel down about the way I look. Believe it or not, I honestly don't. Since embracing I have never felt the need to hate on my body and call it the old names that I used to. 'Ugly' and 'disgusting' are no longer words I use to describe the way I look. Those words are reserved only to describe those who take pride in scrutinising the appearance of others.

I love my body, and it's my mission to help you love yours.

Something about the way you currently feel about your own body has drawn you to this book. Instead of questioning whether I'm worthy enough as a writer to have you here, I'm simply going to do what I do best – share what I have to say.

This isn't rocket science or anything worthy of a Nobel Prize. What I have to say mightn't even be new to you – in fact, if you're like I was, when it comes to body positivity, you've most likely heard every motivational quote and self-help mantra in the book. However, please indulge me. This is *my* book, and I plan on delivering unconditional love for your body a little differently!

So, let's dive in deep. Let's be in this together. Let's help you find your very own golden ticket. Let's get you to embrace yourself . . .

INTRODUCTION

EMBRACE YOURSELF

I'm living proof

If YOU'D TOLD ME TEN YEARS AGO that I'd one day be comfortable taking my clothes off in front of my husband, let alone in front of a room full of strangers, I honestly would have broken out in laughter. The kind of laughter where you imply, through high-pitched inflection, that the person telling you the unimaginable must be seriously out of their minds. Yet, fast-forward a decade and that's exactly where I found myself to be – at a photo shoot, in front of many, wearing nothing but a bikini.

I'm not telling you this to imply it will take a decade to change the way you feel about your body (nothing of the kind, it can happen swiftly!). I'm telling you this because I imagine some people reading this book would be totally able to relate.

Right now, I imagine some of you are in the same achingly painful place that I was in before I embraced. A place of self-loathing, hatred, guilt, shame and embarrassment, with an excruciating desire to change something – or everything – about the way you look.

I remember that when I hated my body, I didn't want to be seen by anyone, let alone my husband, and definitely not by myself in the mirror. Everything I did felt like a battle. The change room was an evil place of misery and despair when trying on clothes, going to the beach I felt embarrassed and ashamed, and – heaven forbid – going to an event where I might run into people I hadn't seen in a long time was an experience filled with fear and trepidation. My life was no life. I was never able to be present in any given situation because I was always filled with negative emotions stemming directly from my pure hatred for my body.

A colleague works on a consumer advisory committee at one of Australia's largest eating disorder associations. She recently shared with me the continual feedback the association receives about a lack of positive role models for people with eating disorders. While helping to draft a pilot program to pair people with eating disorders who are in their final weeks of inpatient treatment with mentors who'd been in recovery for a considerable time, she noted that those in the grips of the illness simply didn't have access to enough success stories to aspire to or believe in. Many within the eating disorder community had never met someone who had recovered from the illness, and not knowing what that recovery 'looked' like made it difficult for sufferers to imagine that a life without fearing food or their weight was possible.

This got me thinking about how important it is for me to let you know that I am here to walk this journey with *you*.

BECAUSE I GET IT.
Boy, do I get it!

Along with inspiring you to find your very own golden ticket to Body Love town, it's also important for me to share with you that I understand how you might be feeling right now. Fat, disgusting, ugly, wobbly – while those words don't leave my mouth these days in relation to my body, they used to form part of my daily inner dialogue. In fact, I probably hated my body more than any of you. Please don't think

I'm saying that competitively. (I mean, seriously, who'd ever strive to feel so hideous?) Rather, I say this to suggest that if I can love my body unconditionally, anybody can. Including you. And you will!

I don't beat myself up about the time I wasted hating my body. Rather than looking back and dwelling on the days gone by, I'd rather look forward to all the fabulous experiences ahead.

Let me share a little of how I used to feel with you.

Hating my body was all-consuming. There was rarely any respite from the awful conversations I'd have in my head. It wasn't always an overwhelming 'I hate my body!' kind of intensity – on many occasions it was like a low-grade temperature, just there, annoying – but it was constant. And crippling.

For example, having sex with my husband, Mat. Rather than be in the moment and enjoy the intimacy of being with the man I love, my mind would race with thoughts like, 'I wonder if he can see my boobs hanging off to the side?' or 'How could he possibly find these tummy rolls of mine attractive?' Not to mention, 'Does my vagina look different since I became a mum?' (I tore a little down there when giving birth to Oliver.)

If I was in a change room, I spent so much time examining the gross roll of fat underneath my bra that sometimes I couldn't even bring myself to try on the clothes I'd taken in there. If I tried on something that didn't fit, I would blame my body for being a complete failure and would begin planning my next diet before even leaving the store.

Most Mondays I began a new diet in order to lose weight from eating 'badly' the week before, always starting off the week determined that I was finally going to be 'good'. When I weighed myself, I constantly felt guilty for not going to the gym enough and wished so badly that I could have 'her' body instead of mine.

I also had a constant monologue going on in my head. *Do I look okay? Is my bottom bigger? Do you still find me attractive? Can you see my back rolls through this T-shirt? Have you noticed I've put on weight? Do you think my face looks bigger? How do these jeans make me look? Are my arms too big to wear this top?* Sound a little familiar?

Hating my body was hard work, as I'm sure many of you would understand. So many of us spend our days bullying our bodies with hurtful language, not to mention engaging in body-shaming activities like these:

- Turning the lights off in the bedroom before getting intimate
- Weighing yourself every day, or trying to lose weight in the lead-up to a special event
- Depriving yourself of food, or constantly counting calories, fat grams or 'points'
- Avoiding sleeveless tops, or wearing shapewear to flatten your stomach, hips or thighs
- Exercising because you *have to*, and spending excessive time in the gym
- Always trying the newest or latest diet fad or product
- Avoiding being seen in a swimsuit at all costs, or covering up as soon you get out of the pool
- Being jealous of 'skinny' friends, and saying negative things about other people's bodies
- Not buying clothes until you lose weight, or keeping clothes that don't fit you because you want to fit into them again one day
- Avoiding having your picture taken, especially full-length photos
- Not leaving the house in fear of what others will think of your appearance
- Telling yourself you are fat and ugly, and that you're 'too fat' to do something

LEARN TO BE

grateful

FOR

your body

AND

your life.

EMBRACE YOURSELF

only this time admiring the pattern of the bikini I was wearing rather than nitpicking my body's condition, I was called over to begin a photoshoot.

'Do you ever have days when you feel bad about your body any more?' the photographer proceeded to ask, while fiddling with camera lenses.

'No,' I replied, matter-of-factly. 'Seriously, I don't!' I added, sensing a little disbelief.

The relationship I have with my body has changed dramatically since I began this journey to embrace. I now place so little value on what my body looks like, and instead value how I *feel* in my body and what my body allows me to *do* so much more.

Think about your legs for a minute. Take a second to stop and think about all the incredible things that your legs do for you, whether they allow you to walk or swim or dance or run. *This* is the way I think about and value my body now. I no longer engage in any form of dialogue that isn't through a lens of my very own – the perspective of gratitude.

Learning to be grateful for your body, and your life, will have a profound impact on your everyday outlook and happiness. It doesn't just happen, I must add – gratitude is a constant practice. Whether you try writing a daily gratitude journal or taking a gratitude meditation, having gratitude and loving your body unequivocally go hand-in-hand. (Kind of like chocolate goes hand to mouth!)

Do you know how hard it is to hate on your body when you've just finished a ten-minute gratitude meditation about how epically fabulous your body is? From the tip of your toes to the top of your head? When you actually stop and reflect on all that your body is (and all that it can do), you can't help but marvel at what an incredibly amazing machine it is!

How about the way your hair stands up on end when it's cold? Or the way the human heart beats over three million times in the average lifespan? Every time you want to complain about something, ask yourself if it's worth your energy. People take their bodies for granted, which may explain why it's so easy to hate them.

I live and breathe the body image conversation every day in my line of work, and yes, being fortunate to connect with body-positive babes around the world fuels the love I have for my body even more. But the Body Image Movement aside, once I stopped viewing my body as an ornament and saw it as the vehicle to my dreams, nothing was going to stop me from developing an unconditional and unwavering love for it.

I am living proof that you can love your body. And not just love it, *adore* it. After all, you only get one – so you'd better get cosy in it!

I'M LIVING PROOF

TWENTY REASONS WHY

I am grateful for my body . . .

1. I love my arms that allow me to hug my children.

2. I love my stomach because my three babies grew in it. It was a pretty great temporary home.

3. I love my legs because they allowed me to run a marathon – and that's a bloody long way!

4. I love my beating heart because, you know, I'd be in trouble without it.

5. I love my eyes that allow me to see people's smiles.

6. I love my ears that allow me to hear music.

7. I love my strong shoulders that allow me to lift heavy weights.

8. I love my fingers that gently type on this computer, connecting the words in my head to thoughts in yours.

9. I love the enormous gap between my big toe and my second toe that gives my friends such a good belly laugh.

10. I love my breasts that fed over 4000 meals to my three children.

11. I love my nose because it can smell all of the delightful essential oils I wear every day.

12. I love my feet because they have balanced me for decades.

13. I love my fingernails because they have been a source of nervous distraction since I was a toddler.

14. I love my clitoris because it allows me to feel delightful pleasure.

15. I love my vocal cords because they allow me to sing in my car and at karaoke.

16. I love my hands because they can hold my daughter's when we walk the dog.

17. I love my little Tic Tac teeth because they chomp through food.

18. I love my tastebuds for allowing me to enjoy flavour.

19. I love my brain that never stops thinking, dreaming and concocting fabulous ideas and thoughts.

20. I love my lungs for allowing me to breathe, especially those long, deep breaths in meditation.

I'M LIVING PROOF

Bang! Kapow! O-M-G!

Most women feel exactly the same way as me!

Jane Gardiner

Body Image Movement Global Ambassador

Growing up, one of the main influences around me was fashion magazines for teenagers that featured the likes of Nicole Kidman on the cover. She was the poster child for how we all needed, or wanted, to look like at the time. She was tall, skinny and had big frizzy hair. I, on the other hand, was curvy and had long straight hair.

At sixteen, I started to become self-conscious about my body. I had developed breasts, which I was extremely embarrassed about, and would wear a tunic dress to school instead of the prescribed shirt and skirt for fear of having the shirt gape open. I would also wear my hair in long pigtails that I'd hang over my boobs to hide them. To this day, I still won't wear a buttoned shirt!

Slowly, over the next thirty-four years, the dislike I had for my breasts moved to other bits of my body, before turning into a loathing that affected my ability to function and socialise. Often it would force me to pull up at the car park, ready for an event or night out, and spend ages trying to convince myself to go in. I would often leave without getting out of the car, and when I did build up the courage to do so, I would put on a happy face despite feeling like I was dying on the inside.

I usually had an excuse for why I couldn't do things, such as having a migraine or feeling unwell, all because I was worried about how I looked and what people would think of me. I missed out on doing activities with my son, for fear of how I looked.

The hatred I had for my body became a constant voice, following me everywhere, whispering, 'You would be so pretty if you just lost some weight.' The self-talk became so ingrained in me that it's only in retrospect that I realise how bad it truly was. I felt very alone, and different to others.

I think when you reach milestones in your life, you start to reflect, and as I approached my fiftieth birthday, I could feel a shift taking place within me.

To begin with, part of my birthday celebrations included a great weekend away with friends. I was at my largest and was feeling apprehensive about the trip. However, when I thought about how much my intelligent, caring and kind friends loved me, I began questioning, 'Why can't I?' I also found a great personal trainer to help me become fitter, and for the first time in my life, I began to focus on exercise for my health – not to lose weight. However, the real light-bulb moment came for me when I first saw the documentary *Embrace*.

I sat in the audience, alone, and a light switched on.

'Bang! Kapow! O-M-G! Most women feel exactly the same as me!'

> Taryn's ability to connect with me and other women worldwide is an absolute gift. Her documentary taught me that while our body image issues may be different, they all stem from a place of perceived flaws and seeking out perfection.

But perfection is driven by the media and marketing departments to make money – it simply doesn't exist – and we are therefore never able to meet the high expectations set for us.

I began devouring all things *Embrace* and the *Body Image Movement*. I read Taryn's *Body Lovin' Guide* and before I knew it, I had applied to become a BIMGA – that is, a *Body Image Movement Global Ambassador*.

Embrace gave me permission to love the bits of my body that I used to loathe. If I do a push-up, I don't have to go as low to the floor as others because I have my pillows out the front! I have been told I give great hugs, so if my arms were not as wobbly as they are, my hugs would not be as squishy and nice!

I do physical activity these days that I enjoy, not for weight loss. I change the type of exercise that I do so I'm not bored and don't allow guilt to influence any of my choices. I'm no longer ruled by my food choices, and I talk to others about my progress and my journey, which helps bolster my confidence and keep me on track.

Now that I embrace
my body, rather than
feel ashamed of it,
I do new things all the
time. If I catch myself
thinking 'I can't'
do something, I push
against it and say,
'Why can't you?'
If my reasoning
doesn't stack up,
I push myself to try it.

I've changed who I follow on social media, only following positive people who make me feel good, and if my friends talk about themselves in a negative way in front of me (or on social media), I will pull them up and get them to rephrase what they think and say about themselves.

I love delivering the message of self-love every day and am proud and honoured to be a Body Image Movement Global Ambassador. I apologise to young people all the time for the way my generation has made them feel about their bodies, because we have all had someone older than us pass judgement on our appearance, be it a family member, teacher, doctor or coach. I also ask everyone I speak with to consider the impact of the words they use to describe their body, particularly when little ears are around.

To embrace your body is to feel a sense of relief. Last summer, I set myself a challenge to walk along the beach in just my swimmers. No sarong or cover-up. Shoulders back, head held high. I discovered that no one cared! No one was interested in me. Most people were just worried about themselves. It was liberating.

Learning to love my body is a work in progress, with thirty-four years of negative self-talk to undo. However, I'm living proof that it's possible. Don't make my mistake – learn to love your body *now*. Find out the things you love, and do them. You will lead the way for the next generation.

What I want for you

Let ME TAKE YOU BACK A FEW YEARS to being in your teens, and being at a club or party when the final song for the night comes on.

If you're like me, right now you're painting the town red in a 1980s Cyndi Lauper–style outfit, about to dance your little heart out to Madonna's 'Holiday'. (However, the choice of song and outfit as you reminisce isn't the point!)

Remember how hard you danced, how you gave that final song your all? Pulling out all your best moves effortlessly in the moment, without a care in the world other than existing in the present? That exhilaration, that feeling of pure joy, is what I want for you. And what's more, I want to help you connect with that feeling often.

I said earlier that when I arrived at a place of loving my body, I felt like I'd won a golden ticket. So what does living with a golden ticket look like?

Besides the obvious spring in your step, twinkle in your eye and dance party in your car on the way to work (or anywhere, really), a life spent embracing all that you are looks joyful and fun. But what is almost inexplicable, and the most important thing about embracing, is how you *feel*. Embracing feels like it's the day after Christmas, when all the craziness subsides, leaving you with nothing more to do than relax, unwind, eat plates of beautiful leftovers in complete comfort and enjoy all the presents you've been spoilt with. It's the feeling of nowhere to be, nothing to do. It's a feeling of absolute bliss.

If bustin' a move to Michael Jackson at a bar wasn't your thing as a teen like it was for me, take a moment to imagine the initial taste of independence you might have felt when riding a bike for the first time, or the sensation of being behind the wheel of a car – without a passenger in tow – experiencing the independence of being mobile and on your own. Oh, the freedom!

Humour me, and imagine going to a local high school fair with your friends and lining up to go on a carnival ride, music blaring through the evening air. The ride assistant is the spitting image of spunky Ponyboy from *The Outsiders*, and straps you into the ride while you enjoy the butterflies in your stomach – the thrill of him, and what's to come! The ride begins, and you fly through the air, forgetting where or who or what you are. You are elated, and when the ride ends, you feel on top of the world. Your head is slightly dizzy; every step is in slow motion.

Imagine the feeling of anticipation and excitement when playing Spin the Bottle at a party, the thrill of winning a game of your favourite team sport with your mates, or laughing uncontrollably at something until you cry tears of happiness. Then there's the moment you get up on skis for the first time, the time your child speaks their lines in a kindergarten play and the adrenaline rush of freefalling backwards on a swing in the air. Oh. The. Joy!

Singing on stage. Rollerskating down a hill. Going for a skinny dip.

WHEN DID YOU LAST
experience real joy?

When you were really young, with such little life experience, you pushed yourself and gave everything your all. You put your hand up, you jumped in, you did more. You rarely cared what people thought, and I imagine there was no one in your head telling you that you couldn't or that you shouldn't. You said yes. You took action. You backed yourself.

When I was little, feeling unselfconscious came naturally to me. Whether it was starting up a new sport or being on stage to dance (with zero dance experience), I'd give anything a go. I'd breakdance at lunchtime with a boom box and gymnastic mats in the school courtyard, not knowing how to breakdance whatsoever! I'd set enormous goals to raise money for charity and compete in swimming carnivals, despite never having trained to swim, because everything seemed possible. Joy was an everyday occurrence.

When I got older, the freedom to experience joy – without guilt – suddenly became something for other people to experience, not me. I couldn't have a piece of cake at morning tea with colleagues because I was a 'pig'. I couldn't swim freely at the beach like other mothers, because I was 'fat and disgusting'. I couldn't go out for an evening meal with my husband and our friends because I looked 'ugly' and 'repulsive'. Everyday experiences that brought happiness to others were somehow reserved, in my mind, for those who had bodies deemed better than mine. The hatred I had for my body robbed me of the freedom to experience life to the fullest.

I can remember going to the beach when my babies were young and instead of being in the moment of playing, splashing, building sandcastles and enjoying the time with them, I would be consumed with thoughts about how I looked. Even when I look back at photos now, of me at the beach with the family, the awful feeling of being self-conscious comes back to me easily. I felt embarrassed, trapped in an ugly body and wishing I looked like the buff mum playing with her son just metres away. I remember the conversations I would have with Mat, always trying to justify how my body looked. I became bitter and mean-spirited, reducing other mothers' bodies I admired to being 'genetically blessed'. I'd say things like, 'Oh, I looked similar to her after having one child – wait until she has three!' or 'I don't know too many people who've had three children in three and a half years – my body never had time to recover.' I dearly love people and believe I had a good heart, so this side of me, produced by my body hatred, was uncomfortable and hard to reconcile.

Do you remember how it felt to be free? Or has it been so long since you last felt a sense of freedom that it's somewhat of a distant memory? Have you lost your joy, or simply want more of it?

Without trying to be too sombre or make you feel even worse than you do about the current state of your sparkliness, palliative care nurse Bronnie Ware says the dying patients in her care often reflect on not allowing themselves the freedom to just 'be': to be happier, and to live their true life.

'This was the most common regret of all,' Bronnie says. 'When people realise that their life is almost over and look back clearly on it, it is easy to see how many dreams have gone unfulfilled. Most people had not honoured even a half of their dreams and had to die knowing that it was due to choices they had made, or not made . . . Health brings a freedom very few realise, until they no longer have it.'

Hang on, hang on! Before your inner voice pipes up and refuses to take accountability for your current state of affairs, remember that you have the power within you, no matter the situation, to change your perspective.

Pretending to be happy, and the fear of expressing otherwise, kept many of Bronnie's patients stuck in particular habits and patterns of behaviours. Many did not realise, sadly, until the end of their lives that happiness *is* a choice. Yes, a choice!

What do I take from all of this? That unless you begin to actively pursue happiness in the present, at the end of your life you'll most likely be lamenting, 'I wish I didn't give a fuck what people thought,' and 'I wish that I'd said "Fuck it" more often'!

I know what you're thinking: 'It's all well and good to sprout from your potty mouth and start effing this and effing that, but that's not a reality.' To some degree, you're right. It's not appropriate to say 'Fuck it' willy-nilly in pursuit of personal joy (I wouldn't recommend up and leaving a classroom full of kids to go throw back a glass of bubbles, for instance), but it is possible to find a balance.

Stop worrying about rocking the boat, stop worrying about what others think, stop worrying that no one will join you on the carnival ride run by Ponyboy. Instead, start worrying about being true to the person you'll be in your final days on this earth. Be true to that person, and what they wanted out of life, and stop settling for a mediocre existence.

So friends, this is what I want for you . . . An exhilarating life that's filled with 'fuck off' and 'fuck it' aplenty!

The current state of play

It WAS WITH SHOCK AND SHEER DISBELIEF that I received over 7000 emails and messages from complete strangers around the world when I posted the trailer for *Embrace*. I always hoped that the documentary would impact the lives of others, but never in my wildest dreams did I anticipate the response to simply sharing the trailer.

Embrace is a film about my mission going out into the world to discover why so many women hate their bodies and what we can do about it. I spoke to experts in the field of body image, photographers, models, a burns survivor and everyday women on the street. In ninety minutes I did my best to try to unpack the why and offer some solutions. I could have made ten documentaries from all of the stories I heard. One thing that absolutely blew my mind was that no matter where I travelled to, body image dissatisfaction had seeped into the minds of every woman no matter what country they were born in or what culture they were raised in.

Night after night once the kids had gone to bed I would sit there on my computer responding to email after email after email from people, all of which had one common message – how much they hated their bodies. As the trailer for *Embrace* got more traction, reading these responses became a nightly routine. Mat would go to bed around ten p.m., kiss me on top of my head and say, 'Don't stay up too late.' And every morning I'd wake, absolutely shattered, having stayed up until the wee hours of the morning attempting to reply to every one of them.

As well as being physically exhausting, it was mentally exhausting too. Reading such sad stories of body hatred night after night was extremely draining, and some of the stories too sad to take:

- 'I've not been intimate with my husband for three years because I think I look disgusting. He tells me he loves me but I just can't bring myself to be naked in front of him.'
- 'I have a four-year-old daughter and I've never swum with her because I don't want to wear a pair of bathers.'
- 'I've been struggling with the way I look ever since I can remember. My mother always reminds me that I'll never find someone who loves me unless I lose some weight.'
- 'I feel so hopeless. I'm trying to learn to love my body but every advertisement, billboard, social media feed convinces me that I'm not good enough.'
- 'I haven't been able to look at myself in the mirror for almost three years. I barely leave the house because I hate being in public where other people can look at me and judge me. My body image issues are ruining my relationships with my friends and loved ones.'

- 'Some days I don't think I can go on because of how
  much I hate my body. How do I learn to love myself like
  you did?'
- 'I've had a difficult relationship with my body ever since
  going through puberty. I compared myself to my friends
  who were all skinnier than me. It quickly developed into
  an obsession with counting calories and losing weight
  and there are days I don't think I can go on.'
- 'I've battled with an eating disorder since I was a teenager.
  It was always a tool for me to control aspects of my life
  whilst I dealt with other trauma.'
- 'I've dieted for years to try and look like what my husband
  wants. I feel like such a failure because I've gained some
  weight back. I'm scared that he will leave me. Please
  help me.'

The state of trauma experienced by those around the world filled me
with despair – so many people feeling so alone, disconnected from not
only their bodies, but from others around them too. So many of the
stories expressed feelings of loneliness and being crippled with pain
brought on by body dissatisfaction, yet each evening I would read a
dozen other identical stories.

I remember the most heartbreaking email I read, from a woman
who had never told her story to anyone before – I was the first person
she was sharing her most intimate secret with. She wrote to me, and said
how she had experienced sexual abuse as a child and never told a soul.
To numb the pain, she ate her way through life, and as a consequence
of emotional eating, she had become overweight ('fat' was her word).
When she walked down the street, she felt judged by the eyes that
gazed at her, and she knew that people thought she was a fat, lazy pig.

But as she explained to me, she was carrying this shame and sadness with her every single day, and food was her only comfort.

She acknowledged that she wasn't physically healthy, but she recognised that she was making an effort to keep on top of her emotional and mental health, 'trying to keep her head above water'. As a single mother to two children, she was just trying to survive.

Oh, the heartache of this story.

Of all the emails I've ever received, this one has had the most impact. I am an empath, which means I feel deeply the emotions of others. It's a gift and a curse sometimes, because the pain of others can bring me to my knees. My eldest son, Oliver, is also an empath, so we can never watch a sad movie together or it becomes the ultimate tear-fest.

It took me days of tears to move on from hearing this woman's story. But what this email did, and the thousands of others too, was give me a sense of responsibility. I couldn't have been trusted with these stories without a purpose, and I couldn't know what I now knew about the heartache experienced around the world and simply do nothing.

I had to respond.

If I thought reading people's emails was hard, hitting the streets while filming *Embrace* and coming face to face with tears and stories of body dissatisfaction in real life was even harder. As I travelled the world, from the Dominican Republic, Austria and the United Kingdom to Germany, the United States and what felt like everywhere in between, I was completely shocked to hear the words that women (and some men) used to describe their bodies.

THE CURRENT STATE OF PLAY

EMBRACE YOURSELF

Fat. Saggy. Chunky. Frumpy. Embarrassing. Hideous. Flawed.
Horrendous. Imperfect. Repulsive. Gross. Ugly. Disgusting.

I'll never forget chatting to a woman from the Dominican Republic. She'd never left the island, and probably never will (her small village didn't even have electricity), and yet when I asked her about the relationship she had with her body, she responded with, 'It's okay . . . but I would like bigger breasts.'

'So, you would like to get cosmetic surgery to get bigger breasts?' I asked her.

'Yes!' she said with enthusiasm. I walked away, utterly sad, because knowing that she would never have the money required to get the bigger breasts she thought she needed, she would forever be unhappy with them and wish for something more.

On the streets in Paris, with a translator for assistance, I stopped a Parisian woman and to my surprise (for some reason I thought French women would feel differently about their bodies) she broke down in tears and talked to me about how much she disliked her body.

Surely the Germans were going to have it sorted? No. Turns out they were as ashamed of their bodies as anyone.

Hang on a second . . . what about all those stories I'd heard about Europeans at the beach with their tops off in summer, worshipping their bodies as much as the sun? What about the French women who were going to be too sophisticated and connected to their fabulous selves to even blink an eye at me as I walked on by? It turns out these are just anecdotal stories we've heard – the truth lies in the tears that I saw every single day of filming when talking to women.

The more I travelled, the worse it became. Before I set out to make *Embrace* I thought I knew how bad the situation was, but I didn't. All the research and statistics in the world cannot prepare you for face-to-face stories of heartache, sadness and despair. Body dissatisfaction was

IF WE
share our stories,
WE CAN
learn,
inspire,
help,
AND
support
ONE ANOTHER.

EMBRACE YOURSELF

truly a global epidemic, and while I wasn't able to visit every country, these disturbing statistics say it all.

In 2015, a study by the International Society of Aesthetic Plastic Surgery (ISAPS) reported that in the single calendar year prior, just shy of 10 million cosmetic surgeries were recorded worldwide and over 21 million non-surgical cosmetic procedures. Of those surgical and non-surgical procedures, the following statistics were revealed:

- 84.7 per cent were performed on women.
- The most popular procedure was breast augmentation, followed by liposuction, eyelid surgery, abdominoplasty and rhinoplasty.
- 95,010 labiaplasty operations were performed.
- 19 per cent of breast augmentation procedures recorded in Brazil were done on women aged 17 years or *younger*.

While these stats are alarming (in particular, the boob jobs being performed on girls), what alarms me even more is the conversations I've had with five-year-old girls who are on diets (whether they used that term or not) and were actively restricting their food intake to lose weight. Equally alarming were the seventeen-year-old girls getting preventive Botox to avoid wrinkles, not to mention the twelve-year-old girls who've stopped playing sport because they don't want to be seen in their swimming costumes. Then there was the conversation I had with a teenage boy, in tears because he hated his 'scrawny body' and was tempted to try steroids, or the seven-year-old girl I met who thought the most important thing to do and be in life is beautiful. I could go on . . .

This all sounds pretty shit, doesn't it?

If I ask all of you reading this book, 'Who feels sad and overwhelmed?'

I'm sure you would all have your hands raised. Collectively we feel the pain of this epidemic. Yet as strange as it may sound, when trying to create a global movement of positive change, this is the moment I get really excited about, knowing I have so many of you on side.

We want to change.

We want to end the war with our bodies, for ourselves and for the next generation. We are all on the same page; it's just that for the longest time we've felt alone. But the lid has well and truly been lifted, and now – for the first time in history – we are connected thanks to social media. We no longer have to endure this pain as individuals. Collectively we can share our stories and learn from one another, inspire one another, help and support one another.

We are often quick to criticise social media. I am guilty as charged, but I think the positive impact it can have far outweighs the negative. If it wasn't for social media, I might still be speaking in a community hall to twelve people!

Asking thousands of strangers on the street how they felt about their bodies when filming *Embrace*, I didn't meet a single person who loved the skin they were in. No one owned the space of loving their body. I'd challenge people's opinions of themselves, and would almost have women declaring with strength and power the love they had for their bodies, but after giving them a few seconds and a moment to pause, they'd follow up any positive statements with, 'but . . .'

Fast forward to now, and I'm slowly beginning to see a shift in the way women talk about their bodies. The body positivity movement is alive

and kicking in every pocket of the globe, with women learning to embrace their bodies and declare that they're not flawed. Women are beginning to appreciate that we are all are unique, equally fabulous, and utterly deserving of self-acceptance and positive self-esteem.

For too long we've been drowning in our destructive body image issues, and I'm glad that women – albeit a small proportion – are finally beginning to forge a new path for generations ahead.

The road to body loving is a courageous one to take, and indeed, sometimes travelling down this path can feel strange and scary and fraught with vulnerability. But I'll tell you what: those who've joined me in embracing know it's a destination like no other. So, take a leap of faith, steer yourself in our direction, and see what all the body positive fuss is about.

Amy D. Herrmann

Photographer for *Underneath We Are Women* project

I want to start by asking a question. Why is a woman's confidence seen as arrogant, and when did self-depreciation become the new modesty? These words have, over time, become mixed up, confused for one another's meanings and intentions. I think it's long overdue that we fixed this.

Three years ago, I embarked on what would be a life-changing journey, a journey in which I would rediscover myself and meet some of the most remarkable women along the way. Unintentionally, I started a community: a community in which women were encouraged and supported to radiate confidence, never confusing it for haughtiness; a community in which modesty didn't mean negative self-talk; a community where women came together in all their diverse glory, and I do mean *actual* glory. Yes, I asked women to literally and metaphorically shed their outer layers and let me photograph them in their most vulnerable and raw, yet most powerful, state.

I called the project *Underneath We Are Women*, and set about photographing 100 diverse bodies to be collected into a book of beauty and power. This journey was not without its ups and downs. These are just a few of the comments I received during the making of this book.

How is being photographed naked empowering women?

What you're doing is sexualising women!

Your children must be so embarrassed!

Hairy Dyke!

Great, let's promote women who cut themselves!

You're promoting obesity!

Gross. Who'd want to fuck that?

So, I pose the following questions:

- How thin does a woman need to be before she's allowed to be seen in public?
- How much do her scars need to fade before she can finally show her arms and thighs?
- Must a naked woman always equate to sex?
- How much do I need to alter my body before a man will want to take me to bed?
- And is the Holy Grail to all of this a man's approval?

Hang on, I didn't realise that my body was actually anyone else's business. And you know what? It isn't! That's the awesome thing about self-love. It is for your*self*.

Here's the thing, I'm not going to wait until my body fits someone else's standards of what a woman should be. Screw that! If you can't keep up with me, then you're the one who's going to be left behind. I will not sit here waiting, stressing, depressing, dieting and missing out on life, simply because my body sits outside of the ever-so-perfect mould created for me by society.

So please, don't quieten yourself to appease someone else's expectations of what they believe a woman should be. Don't self-depreciate under the guise of modesty. You *are* allowed to take up space, and I do mean that in all facets of that phrase. What this project and journey has done to empower women will always outweigh those few wicked comments.

I'll leave you with one last thought – no, fact. My body doesn't exist to please others. This body is *mine* and it does a damn fine job just the way it is!

The highlight reel ain't real

BEFORE THERE WAS THE BODY IMAGE MOVEMENT, there was Sugar Plum Photography.

I know, I *know*, the name sounds pretty naff. I chose a name my dad used to call me when I was little, Sugar plum. (I was his sugar plum fairy, to be precise.)

When Oliver was born, I knew immediately that I never wanted to work for anyone else again. I wanted to stare into his eyes all day, take him on long walks in the pram and incorporate work into *my* life – not the other way around. So when Mat gave me a digital SLR camera for Christmas, my brain started ticking. I could learn to be a photographer! Do a one-hour shoot here and there, get my mum to watch Ollie while I was working, and edit images when he was in bed at night. My small contribution to the mortgage would be sorted and there'd be enough flexibility to never compromise on spending time with my son.

If you're a photographer, please don't shoot me. I know many of you have been to arts school and have done considerable training to be able to work in the field that you do, but guess what? It actually worked out for me! It was the perfect arrangement, and for the first few years (until I decided to shoot weddings – eek!) I scheduled in a handful of family and kids' portraits each week.

I'm not here to verse you in my life history – I won't be writing that book until I'm ninety! – but it needs to be said that while working for Sugar Plum Photography a seed was planted within me to understand the body image epidemic.

At nearly every photo shoot – let's say nine out of ten – I was asked to photoshop the finished images. And let's be straight, I never worked in editorial fashion; I was taking portraits and lifestyle shots of everyday families and women. In front of their children, mothers would say, 'Oh, I hate having my photograph taken. Can you please photoshop my belly a little?' Or 'Can you edit those stretch marks out?', 'Can you get rid of that bit on me there?' and, 'Let's remove those lines around my eyes.'

Ah, what? You want me to take natural photographs of you (my work was known for capturing the natural sunlight of beach and garden settings), but you want me to photoshop the shit out of your face and make you look unreal?

I should probably clarify that this is what I think of the situation now. At the time, I responded pleasingly, and, if in the company of a spouse, would wink cheekily at those asking, implying it'd be our little secret.

Removing dark circles under eyes became one of my specialties, with requests to look younger and thinner the most common. I'm not saying that I retouched every photo, but I certainly did it a lot. And I'm certainly not proud of it. Photoshop is one of the most influential and powerful editing tools in the world. While it seems like the program has been part of our lives and language for an eternity, Photoshop has only existed since 1990. Initially designed as a software package to be used by the technology sectors, the public response was so favourable that the developers worked quickly to release a simpler version of the program for use within other industries.

The editing tool has greatly impacted not only the advertising, film and fashion industries, but it has also had a dramatic impact on the perception we have of ourselves, our bodies and our appearances. According to Jennifer Berger, Executive Director of About-Face, a staggering 95 per cent of the human images we see are retouched, perpetuating unrealistic and unattainable expectations.

During my time running Sugar Plum Photography, I was battling with my own body image issues. I could absolutely empathise with the women wanting to look more 'beautiful', and at the time, I probably would have requested a little editing of my own photos too. Working as a photographer (and sometimes photoshopper) opened my eyes to the sheer scale of society's obsession with perfectionism. These weren't models and cover girls I was editing, or male sport stars starring in endorsement commercials; these were everyday women who felt the need to perfect images of themselves that would later hang in their homes. The pressure to look perfect had, in my eyes, reached a new high.

You only need to watch the scene in *Embrace* where I'm the guinea pig for a photoshopping exercise to see just how quickly and realistically a subject can be transformed into something they're not. And what's more, we've become just as quick to adopt nonchalance towards these kinds of alterations. 'Just photoshop those lines out', 'Just brighten those eyes' and 'Just whiten those teeth' are now colloquial, as though they're okay.

We've glorified the terms hotter, younger, sexier and thinner, so much so that it's no longer enough to ask for the annual family photo we send with our Christmas and Happy Holidays cards to be edited; we want the ability to perfect *every* image we feature in. You don't need to be a professional photographer with the full Adobe suite to manipulate photos these days. All you need is to throw on an Instagram filter and you've lost five pounds, or download a free app to chisel your jawline.

I was speaking to a woman just the other day about this very subject, telling her how I had a pretty big problem with young people being able to manipulate the images they post online. The woman turned to me and said that her daughter only ever changes her skin complexion on Instagram, as if that were a widely accepted and expected thing to do.

She went on to say that every single one of her daughter's images on Instagram had been 'enhanced'. In fact, she'd been told by her daughter that she was not allowed to share any photos of her on her personal accounts unless her skin tone had been smoothed out and she'd personally approved the image for posting. What? Her daughter was only eighteen.

When we see imagery these days, whether it be a family photograph on a wall in someone's home, or on a big billboard in Times Square, for the most part we're being presented with two false realities. First, the image we're seeing has been heavily photoshopped. Second, the image has been painstakingly selected from someone's real life but presented as if it occurred effortlessly. What do I say to that?

- If the model in the photo doesn't even look like the model in the photo, how on earth can *you* expect to?
- Stop comparing your behind-the-scenes to someone else's highlights reel!

There are two issues to address when it comes to image editing.

The first is transparency. I pass no judgement when I say that some people enjoy looking at highly edited imagery, where all surfaces are smoothed, polished and saturated with colour – the incredibly beautiful works of Australian photographer Alexia Sinclair come to mind. What I have a problem with, unlike the justification of artistic expression, is when it's not made obvious to the viewer that an image has been photoshopped.

To begin with, this is deception in its simplest form, and last time I checked, lying to consumers and readers is a criminal act. Why is it that clearly unattainable images of bodies are presented to us as though they can be achieved through exercise, dieting or the latest product a model is selling, when the models don't even look the way they're portrayed?

IF THE
MODEL IN THE PHOTO
doesn't even
look like
THE MODEL IN THE PHOTO,
how on earth
CAN *you*
EXPECT TO?

EMBRACE YOURSELF

A friend and former magazine editor shares the following. 'I stood over our graphic designer when she was working away at a cover shot of Mischa Barton. I instructed her to whiten her teeth, to remove hair wisps, to even her complexion and get rid of wrinkles on her T-shirt. The crazy thing is, as someone who witnessed the entire process happening – the editing, the manipulation – even *I* was fooled when I saw the finished magazine hit the stands. I wanted so desperately to look like Mischa Barton, with flawless skin and perfect hair. If I bought into the hideous deception of it all, what hope would your everyday consumer have of not being sucked in?'

Scarier still is research conducted by Dr Marilyn Bromberg, Senior Lecturer in Law at the University of Western Australia. She has found that everyday women, not just magazine editors, are now easily able to identify whether or not an image has been photoshopped, but still, the ideal presented is detrimental. Together with Cindy Halliwell of the University of Melbourne Law School, Marilyn has devised what they call their Body Image Law.

'How often have you seen a photo of a skinny model and wished that you looked like her – when she may not actually look like that? Photoshopping models to make them appear thinner is prolific and problematic,' Marilyn says. 'Health researchers have found that when people see these images, they compare themselves to the models, and if they find that they are larger, this can contribute to poor body image. Body Image Law was created to combat this: for example, Israeli and French governments passed laws that require a warning on these images. More governments should consider following suit, if the laws are successful.'

I agree wholeheartedly.

The second issue with editing imagery is the fierce societal desire to be 'perfect'.

As a mother to a young daughter, it really bothers me that I can't even take Mikaela shopping without feeling the need to protect her from exposure to the unobtainable and celebrated models on posters in the shopfront windows.

I remember last Christmas, walking hand in hand with Mikaela through a shopping centre, and constantly attempting to distract her from looking at various objectified imagery – all heavily photoshopped, of course. I don't want Mikaela to grow up desiring perfect skin, because what happens if she becomes a pimply teenager? Is she meant to feel crap because the only skin shown in images, magazines, shopfronts, brochures and catalogues is smooth and rendered to perfection?

I don't want her to think that something is wrong with her if she has cellulite but only sees images of women without it. I don't want her to think something is wrong with her teeth because they are not blinding white, or that her breasts aren't big enough because they don't fill out a bikini. I don't want Mikaela on the treadmill of seeking out perfection – I've been there – and I don't want her desiring to be anything other than what she is, because it's exhausting. I don't want this for you either.

What advice do I have for those wanting to look 'picture perfect'?

START WORKING ON

how you feel.

Do you know how many times a man asked me to remove his dark circles or shave a little bit off his waist? Guess. That's right, not once!

In the history of Sugar Plum Photography I never received a request from a single man wanting to change a part of his body.

In no way am I saying that men are immune to body image issues (in fact, there's content enough in that issue for me to write another book!), but there was a definite discrepancy between men and women. Why? Because the men I photographed – everyday blokes and dads – had an absolute ball with their wives and their kids on the day, and their joy was reflected in their photos. When they saw the pictures I'd taken, they didn't see age spots or thinning hair. They were transported to the memorable time in which it was taken.

How do you improve how you feel in front of a camera, and star in images that remind you of wonderful times (not wrinkles and lines)? Here are three steps to apply the next time someone asks to take your picture.

step 1
Say, 'Yes!'

step 2
Look at the camera.

step 3
Smile.

Or you could take a leaf from the book of one of my all-time favourite human beings, Celeste Barber. Heck, she doesn't just get in front of the camera and smile, she takes it to another level with her infectious, parody-style images that truly make the world a better place. (If for some reason you don't know who Celeste Barber is, please follow her immediately on social media – you will thank me later!)

I caught up with Celeste recently (and did my best to not drool on her – after all, humour is for me the most attractive characteristic

in another human being), and asked her about the commotion she has created online. With over 3.5 million followers on Instagram alone, she is the queen of highlighting how the highlight reel ain't real. This is what she had to say:

'So, it turns out I'm a massive deal online, for something that I never would have expected.

'I'm a trained actor. I'm a writer and a comedian. I'm a mother and a wife. I went to State for javelin in Year 8. But that's not why people know me. I'm known because I'm Brave.

'Now, you could be forgiven for thinking I'm brave because I survived emergency open-heart surgery at twenty-five, or because I have been a step-parent since the age of twenty-one, or because I did my first poo after naturally delivering my children without tearing, but you would be sorely mistaken, my friends. I have developed a large following because I put my unconventional hot body into ill-fitting underwear with the sole purpose of making people laugh. Not to body shame, not to compare how I look with other women, but to make people laugh.

'And I don't think this is brave. I think this is normal. It's real. It's healthy. I believe that how we look makes up a very small percentage of who we are, and that "body shaming" and "healthy living" are being sold to us as the same thing. They aren't the same thing. They aren't The Veronicas: identical twins with a few quirky differences. They are completely different beings. One is mean and from a rich bullying family, and the other is a nice guy who helps out at home and likes to make people smile.

'It's important to realise that these two industries are completely different, and to start giving me credit for my javelin skills.'

BEAUTY IS NOTHING
YOU CAN SEE. BEAUTY IS
humility, kindness, humour and compassion.

EMBRACE YOURSELF

Embrace ~~Express~~ yourself

E

MBRACE THE DOCUMENTARY WAS FUNDED BY 8909 PEOPLE. To give
you some context, that's eight times the number of people who
went to my high school. I don't think I've even met 8909 people
in my life, let alone called on that many people for support. Yet when
I wanted to make a documentary exploring the global body dissatisfaction
epidemic, that's exactly what happened.

Embrace was one of the world's most successfully crowd-funded
documentaries – and in Australia in 2016, the most successful in history.
Who would have thought, sitting at my dining room table with a pile
of washing and three young children, that when I uploaded the slightly
cocky campaign title ('EMBRACE – the documentary that will create
global change') that 8909 people would take a punt on my vision.

I'd never made a documentary before, and in those early days
I had no idea how difficult the process was going to be. Documentary-
and filmmakers know how challenging a feature film is to make. In fact,
I'm sure they would have rolled their eyes at my lack of experience
when diving in head first. When I set out on the adventure I assumed my
years telling stories through photography would put me in good stead.
Let's just say, I ate a fair share of humble pie during the experience.

Making *Embrace* was intense, stressful and took twelve months
longer than initially planned, with the stress manifesting into a giant
cold sore that nestled in on my face for around two years. I now

apologise to every filmmaker I meet – 'Oh, yeah, by the way, sorry that I was such a knob for thinking that filmmaking would be a walk in the park.' But in hindsight, thank goodness I thought it would be easy, because if I'd fully appreciated the responsibility of fulfilling the belief of 8909 people, I probably would have run and hidden instead!

I'm very proud and grateful that the film has lived up to its expectations. It's changing people's lives, and I couldn't be happier. But my goodness, it took a village to get the film to what you see on the big screen today. So many committed people behind the scenes, not to mention Mat and the rest of my family, gave it their all – and with so much emotion too. From the film's producers and editors to music composers, graphic designers and those on screen, everyone involved – including myself – learnt so much about body acceptance and celebration that I thought I'd share a little of that with you now.

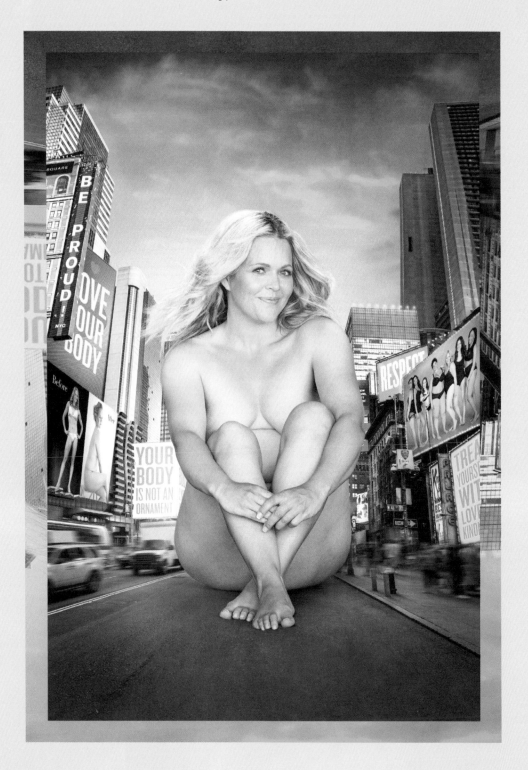

EMBRACE YOURSELF

EMBRACE YOURSELF

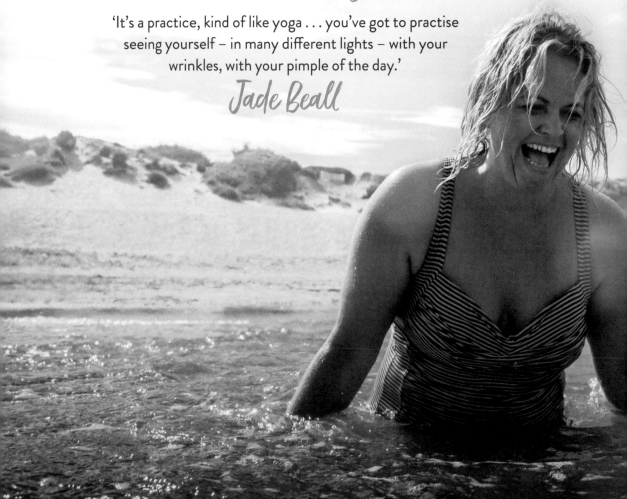

'I look in the mirror and I pinch my arm, and I just wonder what it would be like to be one of those women that could just get over it – just be okay with what I have today . . . It's a real struggle and I resent the fact that so many days and hours and time has been spent hating what I look like.'

Ricki Lake

'You can either be depressed about this the rest of your life, or you can figure out a way to still continue to shine the brightness that you are inside . . . We get to define what true beauty is, what it's like to really feel comfortable in our own skin, what it's like to have a positive body image . . . It starts with people accepting others the way that they are.'

Renee Airya

'It's a practice, kind of like yoga . . . you've got to practise seeing yourself – in many different lights – with your wrinkles, with your pimple of the day.'

Jade Beall

'Now – being in the state that I am, and that I love my body and
I'm proud of it – I can focus on more important things in life.'

Stefania Ferrario

'I'd get to the end of these magazines and realise I wasn't tall enough,
I wasn't skinny enough, I wasn't blonde enough. I just wasn't enough . . .
If you're always comparing yourself to something that doesn't actually exist,
how can you possibly feel good when you look in the mirror?'

Mia Freedman

'We are all so different. We need to celebrate the fact we are different . . .
Love your bodies for the way that they are because your body
is the only body that you have.'

Harnaam Kaur

'If I want to eat the fucking cookie my kid baked,
I'm gonna eat the fucking cookie my kid baked.'

Amanda de Cadenet

EMBRACE YOURSELF

A lot of really incredible things have happened to me and the Body Image Movement over the past five years, with one of the highlights being the new people I've met who've since turned into lifelong friends.

During the crowdfunding campaign on Kickstarter, I became somewhat keyword obsessive, incessantly hitting F5 to refresh the campaign page and see the funds being raised. The way Kickstarter works is that you must meet the designated amount in sixty days – in the case of *Embrace*, that was $200 000 – or the campaign is unsuccessful. That's right, you could be sitting at $190 000 with two hours to go, and unless that final $10 000 is donated, you'd walk away with little more than RSI.

The campaign had a large number of backers, so contributions would trickle in, often ranging anywhere from $1 to $200. I spent most of those sixty days staring at my computer screen pensively, imagining what I would do if I didn't hit the target. So you can picture my absolute shock after refreshing the page one day to see a whopping $8000 having just been donated.

'Mat! Mat! Mat! MAT!' I shrieked with delight. 'Someone has just contributed $8000!'

I immediately went into the back end of Kickstarter to investigate and saw that a woman by the name of Nora Tschirner had supported the project. I had no idea who she was, but sent her a message of thanks the very same day. I googled her name out of interest, and was both shocked and excited to learn that she was a German actress and, therefore, the campaign had reached Germany!

Nora sent a delightful email back to me and we decided to Skype. Like someone about to embark on a blind date, I was a little unsure of how the digital meet and greet would transpire, but within thirty seconds of her online company, I had fallen head over heels in friendship with her. She was very much my spirit animal – slightly kooky, very funny, very

friendly, super intelligent and super down-to-earth. I also learnt there was no motive involved, only a desire to help women the world over learn to accept their bodies more.

Nora's profile in Germany is big (what Julia Roberts is to America) and her contribution sparked a lot of interest by other Germans. Before too long, the campaign had ended and we'd reached the target (and then some).

EMBRACE THE DOCUMENTARY

was going to be made!

Now, what would a chapter about the documentary be without spilling a few secrets from behind the scenes? There were no off-screen catfights or competition between the stars of the film. However, I'll see if I can make some of the following documentary insights just as juicy!

I DID MY HOMEWORK.

If I had a dollar for the number of times people said how lucky I was that the crowdfunding campaign did so well, I probably could have funded the film myself! It drove me crazy to hear, because little did people know that I studied Kickstarter for six months prior to executing my campaign. Sure, campaign headquarters were at my dining room table with small people everywhere, but luck played no part in its success. Bloody hard work, planning and preparation did.

MAKING A FILM IS EXPENSIVE.

The film's budget blew out to just over $900 000. Oops! And I must add, it wasn't because I chose to stay in swanky hotels when filming across the world, nor was it because I took an entourage or requested to be driven by a chauffeur in nothing but a Bentley. It turns out that filmmaking, including lawyer's fees and broadcasting rights, is very expensive!

Thank goodness for the likes of incredible human beings like Jude Perl, the artist whose songs, including 'Hungry & Horny' and 'Embrace', breathe life into the film. I met her in the green room of a television studio, right before I was to appear on morning TV, and immediately fell in love with her style. She was being interviewed before me so we got chatting, and it turned out her music was the most perfect fit for the documentary. She offered her songs as a gift to the film.

I EXPERIENCED ANXIETY WHEN FILMING.

When filming in New York City, I experienced anxiety for the very first time. It left me panicked, frightened and very upset in a hotel room on my own, and was one of the worst experiences of my life. Regardless of whether or not you believe yourself to be superwoman, able to travel to six countries in a week, there are going to be some consequences. The fear of feeling this level of anxiety again stays with me, even today.

I found myself experiencing anxiety again during filming when in Germany. I tried handling it a little differently than I did in New York, posting the following on social media:

So I've been feeling really bad for the past 24 hours. Yes, I am unstoppable, but wham bam, last night, like a freight train, I was hit with a serious dose of homesickness that manifested itself quickly into anxiety and feelings and thoughts I've never experienced.

I felt like the four walls of my hotel were closing in on me. I found it hard to breathe, and all I wanted was my family. I'm no stranger to travel, but perhaps being in an unfamiliar city with a very hectic travel schedule (seven countries in three weeks) and being away from my family for more time than I've ever been set it all off.

Making the best doco that I can is what I am here to do, so desperate times called for desperate measures! Hugging is my 'thing'. I love feeling connected to people, and with no one around that I know to hug, I thought, 'What am I going to do?'

So this is what I did [see next page]. And guess what? The people of Berlin hugged me back and I felt a hundred times better!

The world needs more love, and hugging might just be the answer . . . so embrace, people – Embrace!

Wearing a sandwich board, much like a late-night seller trying to promote souvlakis, I had donned a sign offering free hugs to anyone who would oblige me. And do you know what? It worked!

YOU CAN'T WIN 'EM ALL . . .

Embrace was invited to the Sydney Film Festival and the New Zealand International Film Festival. However, it was rejected from the AACTA Awards in Australia, the LA Film Festival, the London Film Festival and Toronto Film Festival. Boo!

BUT WHEN YOU DO WIN, IT FEELS FANTASTIC!

Embrace beat the likes of *King Arthur: Legend of the Sword*, from BAFTA-nominated director Guy Ritchie, and *Guardians of the Galaxy* to claim the number-one spot at the German box office!

When the time came to plan the release of *Embrace* into Germany, Nora recommended a friend of hers who was an independent distributor. Nora had several meetings with them in my absence, meaning I could stay in Australia with Mat and the kids. The release plan they devised was unique and bold – to release *Embrace* into cinemas across Germany for one night only. There was an element of risk to this release, putting all our eggs in one basket, but with Nora spending the weeks leading up to my arrival doing interviews for several magazines, newspapers and TV shows, I had the feeling it was going to work.

A few days before the premiere (and finale!), I flew over to join Nora in Berlin for some publicity. She met me at the airport and was holding a huge sign that read 'CAUTION: I'm going to Embrace the shit out of you in 10, 9, 8 . . .'

It was so nice to get off a plane after travelling for over twenty hours to be greeted by a big sign, a bunch of flowers and a warm hug.

No anxiety in sight.

Thanks largely to the incredible support of Nora, the film struck a serious chord with over 52 000 people across Germany and Austria who turned out to watch the film debut in a theatrical one-night-only release. That's right, 52 000 people watched *Embrace* in one night!

I'm still trying to process and digest the enormity of what happened, that an Australian documentary could reach number one in a foreign country. But it did! The film topped box office charts, taking in €476 746 (approx. AU$713 000) in a single evening, and became one of the most successful Australian films in history to be released there.

IT BLOODY WORKED.

While we kicked some goals in terms of numbers and records with
Embrace, what really makes my heart sing is that the film will be a catalyst
for so many of those sitting in cinemas, lounge rooms and classrooms to
commit to unconditionally loving their bodies.

As an Australian, I'm quite fond of an underdog story and that's
exactly what *Embrace* was. For a foreign film in many of the countries it
was released in, and a documentary on body image no less, to be supported
and (for want of a better word) 'embraced' was beyond my wildest
imagination.

I've always believed in the power of people coming together,
from the bottom up, and the magic we can make when working together.
It just takes one person – like me – to make that initial spark that will ignite
a fire in the bellies of others.

If you have a dream, as I did, to make positive and impactful change
in the world (or have a dream in general, actually!) and it seems so big that
it scares you, go for it. Embrace yourself. Leading up to the Kickstarter
campaign, I had a lot of people tell me I was aiming too high. While
their unwavering support would have been lovely, the person I needed
to convince the most was myself. And once I believed in myself – once
I embraced myself – before I knew it, 8909 people had backed me too.

EMBRACE YOURSELF

FUCK OFF!

CAN'T BELIEVE I've called one of the chapters in this book 'Fuck Off!' But to be honest, I just can't think of a better way to describe one of the greatest and most courageous life lessons I need to share with you.

Now before I go any further, I suppose I should tell you what it is I encourage you to say 'fuck off' to. And in the spirit of this book, being completely inclusive and all, if you find the f-word too hard to imagine integrating into your daily vocabulary, feel free to substitute the expression with an almighty 'piss off', 'beat it' or 'go away'. Nothing has quite the same punch as 'fuck off', though. Just sayin'.

What am I telling you to say 'fuck off' to? The many messages that you receive every day telling you to be anything other than what you are.

Fuck off to all the messages in the world telling me to be something else.

Sound boring? I promise you this chapter is anything but. You may think you understand where the messages you hear about body image are coming from, but I guarantee you've underestimated the sheer amount of messaging you're subjected to daily.

Messaging comes in many forms, from ads on television and billboards to online magazines and social media, not to mention friends, family and sometimes strangers. You'd be familiar with the messages you hear via these avenues, and in fact entire books are dedicated to the messages going on around you. So I'd like to bring your attention to some

EMBRACE YOURSELF

mediums you may not even realise feature forms of messaging.

In our household, each morning is a colourful and chaotic sequence of calamities as we go from our beds to the breakfast table to the bathroom and out the door to begin the drive to work and school. In that time – let's say an hour – my kids and I are likely to have seen over a hundred individual messages. Told you this wasn't boring!

The alarm goes off and straight away I'm presented with the message that the early bird catches the worm and that I *must* get out of bed to begin the daily grind. I step out of bed and put on my slippers and dressing gown, because A) for some reason I've been told that other shoes simply won't suffice for this time of day, and B) that rather than put on a cardigan or jumper, I must have a specific item to perform the job of providing warmth in the morning (again, these are messages I've been given).

Fast forward to the breakfast table, where there's skim milk with a pale-pink logo for me – because as an adult woman, full fat is *not* an option – and full-cream milk with dark-blue stripes for the hubby – because y'know, he's a bloke and needs the energy. (Take a look at how skim and full cream are advertised next time you're at the supermarket – the messaging is pretty clear about which kind of milk is meant for whom!) The three kids have full cream, but soon Mikaela will join me in drinking the low-fat milk when she starts developing and needs to 'watch' her weight.

And then cereal? Sheesh, don't even get me started on the messaging there! Cereal boxes are some of the worst culprits for negative and prescriptive messaging. Not only are breakfast cereal boxes plastered in 'low-fat', 'no-fat', 'gluten-free', 'low-carb', 'sugar-free', 'high-fibre' and 'energy-rich', but cereals aimed at children are one of my pet peeves. (I imagine it's the same for many parents.) Appealing cartoon characters, free gifts, colourful designs, large fonts and the television commercials that go with them make sugary cereals almost impossible to keep from your children's gaze. And does the intended messaging work? You bet it does!

FUCK OFF!

I'M

perfect

JUST THE WAY

I am.

EMBRACE YOURSELF

Try walking down a cereal aisle with three kids and leaving without either having had an argument about why a bowl of sugar for breakfast isn't helpful or a trolley full of fruit hoops.

I recently came across a figure from one of my favourite documentaries, *Miss Representation*. The estimated number of commercials the average American girl has seen by the age of twelve is 77 546. Now, that's *a lot*. A hell of a lot. And if we consider the advertising we're exposed to, I think it's fair to say that most of the messages this young girl has heard aren't about loving who you are or what you were born with – they'll have been about making her feel insufficient without a particular product someone is trying to sell. Essentially, she's being told she is 'not enough'.

Now, it's easy to get angry, especially when you estimate the number of ways you're told to be anything but who you are each day, but let me make it clear that I'm not suggesting you tell people to their faces to fuck off. Not at all! And when I use the term 'Fuck off', it's not meant to be said in an aggressive or mean-spirited way. It's more of an attitude.

Last week I was reading a local lifestyle publication that had a ten-page wedding special at the back. Out of those ten pages, one was a full-page advert from a plastic surgeon encouraging brides to 'Start your wedding plans with us!' Yep. Along with flowers, a cake, photography and a reception venue, brides-to-be now need to be adding plastic surgery to their pre-wedding planning list too! The ad suggested that brides come in for a free consultation with a cosmetic nurse, and to bring a friend or even their mum! Because getting injections in your face and slicing your body open is just as memorable and special as going wedding-dress shopping with the mother-of-the-bride – clearly.

No. No. No! Surgery is a big deal, and so is injecting chemicals into your body, so a woman's decision to have surgery should not be presented in the same vein as deciding on a chai tea or a soy latte. Just because there is an injectable clinic on every street corner does not mean it isn't a big deal.

While I've decided against any cosmetic enhancing surgery for myself, this is not to say that I judge those who decide to go ahead with it. I don't think all surgery is bad. In fact, a lot of my friends have had surgeries and regular Botox, which makes them happy. My issue with cosmetic surgery is that people think it's the *only* alternative to finding happiness with your body if you are currently dissatisfied. It's not. There is another alternative, and it's my life's work to educate (and hopefully inspire) women to get off the beauty treadmill and instead value themselves for who they are, what they do and how they feel!

The magazine I read, and the message of needing surgery, was simply one that I chose to begin this conversation with you. There are thousands more messages designed to impact the thought patterns of women. As a little social experiment at the hairdressers recently, I grabbed the pile of magazines in front of me and wrote down all of the messages I received from their pages. Here are just a few of them – and unfortunately, by a few I don't mean three . . .

FUCK OFF!

LOOK SEXY NOW!

NIP, TUCK

Stop ageing now!

The truth behind how to do it.

Lose 30 pound.

GET SMOOTHE SKIN IN THIRTY MINUTES

TEN TOTALLY GORGEOUS NEW HAIRSTYLES . . .

BECAUSE EVERY WOMAN DESERVES MAN-MAGNET HAIR.

THE NEW WAY SHE STAYS SO SLIM!

How I lost 10lb
HER SEXY BOD
The *easy diet & worke*

A TIGHTER TUMMY IN ONE WEEK – *WITHOUT EXERCISE!*

5 WAYS GET TH SEXIE BODY POS PREGNAN

BOTOX BREAKTHROUGHS:
the new discovery that goes beyond erasing wrinkles.

YOUR FASTEST WAY TO LOSE WEIGHT

A BETTER BODY IN TWENTY-FOUR HOURS

Her *SEXY* body is back
The easy diet and workout that did it!

GET A *SEXY* SIXPACK!

SLEEP YOUR WAY SLI
WHY MISSING ZZZ'S CAN MAKE YOU

Your fastest way to lose weigh

R NOT?

ast!

GET A
WHOLE
NEW LOOK
THIS YEAR!

DIET ALERT!

WHY EATING
HEALTHY IS
MAKING YOU FAT!

10 SUPER-EASY WAYS TO LOOK YOUNGER FAST

THE BEST MAKEOVERS:
*Experts reveal the fast and easy ways
you can make a dramatic transformation.*

THE LATEST INNOVATION
FAST FAT MELTERS!

DROP
POUNDS
IN DAYS!

n 10 days!
S BACK!
at did it.

Eat, drink & still shrink

START TODAY!

Four weeks to
your best butt.

HOW TO
STAY BEACH
READY YEAR
ROUND!

KILLER THIGHS: GET'EM IN THREE *EASY* MOVES!

FLAT ABS FAST!

the secret surgery:
LOOK YEARS YOUNGER IN 60MINS OR LESS

The all-natural tummy tuck

ARE
ANY
WEIGHT
LOSS
PILLS
SAFE?

DROP 2 SIZES!
EASY PLAN   FAST RESULTS
THE EASY DIET AND WORKOUT THAT DID IT.

my body is back!
No gimmicks.
No surgery!

ULTIMATE
CELEBRITY
TONE-UP PLAN

My goodness,

DOESN'T THAT
FEEL EXHAUSTING?!

Is it any wonder that so many women hate their bodies, with these endless messages coming at them?

If you think you might be immune to the messages because you don't read magazines, they'll get to you some other way. Like when I went to purchase a pair of fitness leggings and the sales assistant said, 'No good. They're a little wrinkly and too big in the legs. But the good news is that you've lost some weight.'

Why, thank you, idiot.

That's just one example where unwanted messages have been thrown at me like sand in my face at the beach. I have a lifetime of stories and comments that I've collected, dating back to when I was only a little girl. I remember being praised for being pretty. We are doing a great disservice to young girls if we set the foundations of their self-esteem in looking pretty and valuing their appearance – and it isn't going to help them develop a healthy body image.

The unavoidable messages are loud and clear that you need to change everything about how you look to feel better . . . and this is where the 'fuck off' comes in! You see, it's *your* choice how you perceive the messages and what you choose to do as a result of being confronted with them.

When I hated my body, I would walk through a shopping centre and see a 'hot' woman in a poster in a bikini and wish I had a body like hers.

I would see the flawless skin of the women in advertising campaigns for skincare and wish that I had their skin. Now when I shop, I still see the same images, but they don't have a negative impact on me because I see them for what they really are – misrepresentations of all that it means to be a woman.

Women are smart, intelligent and fabulous, with so much to contribute to the world, yet so many of us are anchored down by thoughts we have about ourselves, because we are on a treadmill. The treadmill of beauty, youth and perfection. We come in all shapes, sizes, ethnicities and abilities but we just don't see it.

So, we have a choice.

We can either let this misrepresentation own us or we bow out of the race by saying 'Fuck off'. We exercise our right to not buy into the bullshit. We are taking back our power.

When we say 'Fuck off!' to all of the messages that don't make us feel good – the messages that don't serve us – it not only *feels good*, it creates so much space in your brain and so much energy in your body. It's only after you've taken yourself off the treadmill that you realise how much time you've actually wasted on it.

People often ask me how I find the time to do all the things I do. Well, I have the same amount of time in my day as anyone else, but the difference is that I don't spend time obsessing, worrying and experiencing mental trauma about my body. It's this feeling of freedom that drives everything I do.

FUCK OFF!

AND THIS JOY AND FREEDOM IS
what I want for you!

Jes Baker

Body positive activist and author of *Landwhale*

A few years ago, I found myself sitting on a couch in New York City in front of an overflowing audience of plus-size women, rubbing shoulders with the Director of Getty Images and Yahoo Style's Editor-in-Chief. The three of us were flanked by other fashion professionals including a famous photographer, the global brand president for a clothing company and the stylish interviewer who had brought us all together to talk about size representation in the plus-size fashion industry.

I couldn't help but wonder where the hell the conversation was going to go as all the panellists came from such divergent backgrounds, and only *two* of us were visibly plus-size. While I'd love to share my clever (and cutting) comments about how fatphobia is still the reason 'plus' women have comparatively fewer fashion options (and how these ruffled some very prominent feathers on the panel), I think the greatest comment to share with you came from another panellist.

The Director of Getty Images essentially said that consumers are no longer looking to companies for trends, but rather, companies are looking to their consumers for inspiration. This was something I had known for quite a while, but to hear it corroborated by a 'professional' in a public forum was nothing short of thrilling. It had been said. Recorded. Documented. Absorbed by the masses in person. *We*, the consumers, were gaining power when it came to voicing (and, in a perfect world, receiving) what we want and need.

We internalise thousands of media messages a day (all created to elevate consumerism), often selling us the idea that we are embarrassingly inadequate and [fill in the blank company name] can fix it! (But only if you give them all of your money.) This is easily done through channels of blatant advertising or, perhaps the most effective tactic, through purposeful exclusivity.

Creating a calculated lack of representation leaves us with a subconscious message that those who *do not* appear do not deserve to be seen, and while many companies are now

changing their exploitative approach by touting their 'inclusiveness' in their advertisements, the positive change (if any) has been minimal. We still have a long way to go.

I first experienced the power of challenging bullshit advertising in 2013 when I spoke up against comments that Abercrombie & Fitch CEO Mike Jeffries had made in 2006. Jeffries's declaration about the Abercrombie & Fitch target market, though several years old, had resurfaced and fuelled worldwide outrage in a way it hadn't before: 'Candidly, we go after the cool kids. We go after the attractive all-American kid with a great attitude and a lot of friends. A lot of people don't belong [in our clothes], and they can't belong. Are we exclusionary? Absolutely.'

This statement, combined with the company's refusal to offer women's clothing in size extra-large, brought enormous and unwelcomed attention to the brand, and quickly became a repeated news headline.

The concept that fat women aren't attractive or worthy of inclusion was what needed to be addressed, and it seemed only appropriate to challenge that assumption by using the style of the brand's overtly sexual advertisements. I teamed up with a local photographer and 'traditionally attractive' model John Shay, and one sunny morning, I got sexy with a guy that the world told me I couldn't.

I wrote an open letter, attached the photos (some were half nude, some wearing a large Abercombie & Fitch shirt that *actually* fit) and published it.

Twelve hours later, I was on a red-eye flight to New York City for an interview on the *Today Show*, and I then proceeded to spend the next twenty hours (no exaggeration there) in a hotel room doing interviews for nearly every major news platform in the world.

People were both cheering and booing; shouting in celebration of size inclusion and hollering about the offensiveness of fat bodies being presented unapologetically. All of the reactions were beneficial, because these sexy black-and-white images (with the Abercombie & Fitch logo changed to 'Attractive & Fat') were forcing the world to see a fat and culturally reviled body in a new light. The effect of seeing images like this? Well, it can change the world.

A 2012 study by scientific journal PLOS ONE noted that there seemed to be a discrepancy in what type of body (especially in regard to weight) Western culture prefers as compared to other parts of the world. What's more, this discrepancy wasn't necessarily attributed to 'biological attraction'. Could it possibly be because we're force-fed one example of the perfect woman? Well, yes! So, what happens when we change the body that is shown repeatedly?

Lynda Boothroyd, a psychology researcher at Durham University in England, who led the study, explains. 'Changing negative attitudes about body size might be as simple as changing what you see. When women in England were shown photos of plus-sized women in neutral grey leotards, they became more tolerant . . . Showing them thin bodies makes them like thin bodies more, and showing them fat bodies makes them like fat bodies more.'

What does this all mean? It means we are retrainable. Our brains can be reconditioned. All is not lost. We have the opportunity to change the world, guys. If we actively feed ourselves visual proof of the diversity that exists in our world, we *will* learn to appreciate all bodies for what they are.

Here's the best part. We can all contribute to taking this study's findings and amplifying the effects by simply posting unaltered photos of ourselves on the internet.

Up until the social media age, our visual measuring sticks were dictated to us by marketing and advertising companies. We saw what they put in front of us – on television, in the movies, in online campaigns and in magazines. But now, just as the panellist I shared the couch with said, *our* voices are becoming the most important part of the conversation.

This is why I wholeheartedly support selfie culture. While criticised by some as narcissistic, selfies are actually one way to participate in an effective tactic that many activists use within their movement: culture jamming. Culture jamming is a visual way to disrupt or subvert mainstream cultural systems. Of course, this includes corporate advertising, and it's something each and every one of us can do!

Every time we share unedited, authentic and 'real' photos of ourselves on a public platform, we are essentially saying, 'This is *me*, world! Whatcha gonna do about it?!' It's a practice of self-care and it can be a powerful experience for each of us.

We post, watch and perhaps receive some kind words from friends, but we also get to enjoy the pleasurable experience of not 'dying' from the body shame that we may have anticipated before pushing the 'post' button. But it's important to remember that there is an even bigger outcome that comes from selfie culture. We are flooding the internet with our diversity.

Companies are no longer the only ones dictating the bodies we see. *We* play a part in that narrative too. We are leading the body image conversation more than ever before. It's a unified and visually staggering middle finger to a culture that has attempted to tell us who we are and what we're worth. With every upload, we get to say, 'Fuck off! I'm perfect just the way I am!'

We may have a long way to go before any large system is fully toppled, but know that when each and every one of us offers proof of our authentic selves, we are collectively changing a conversation that we have forced our way into – whether companies like it or not. And that, my friends? That's some powerful shit I hope we all intend to use.

Eat glitter for breakfast...

WHAT HAPPENS WHEN YOU SAY 'FUCK OFF'? You have the ability to say 'Fuck it!' and strive for something better.

This concept is by no means a scientific theory, obviously! Rather, it is a Taryntific concept for which I am the poster child, and you'll simply need to trust me on it.

I recently introduced this 'fuck off' and 'fuck it' concept to those outside my family for the very first time, at a conference. I was racked with nerves in the days leading up to this as it would be the first time I introduced such a bold concept. Oh, did I mention that the 500-strong audience was made up of accountants? Eek! As a keynote speaker, there is a lot riding on your short presence on stage and it was a bold move to deliver a new talk – especially to an unfamiliar audience.

About seventy-two hours before I was due to speak, I sat down with a blank piece of paper and was just about to rewrite my presentation when something struck me like a bolt of lightning. In a moment of clarity and free of fear, I said, 'Taryn! You want to teach people to say "Fuck it" and do more, push their boundaries, extend themselves out of their comfort zone, and yet you can't even extend this to yourself? C'mon, girl. Move on. Fuck it and do it!' So I did.

I was the last speaker due to present, and the two speakers before me were phenomenal. One just so happened to have been the Young Australian of the Year, and the other a runner-up! I wanted to run and hide, with the pressure of the performance so high it felt like a thick turtleneck underneath my jaw. My heart was racing and my palms were sweaty, and as I walked up the steps towards the lectern, all I could think was, 'Taryn, fuck it. Taryn, own it. Taryn, fuck it.'

I did! And the audience loved it. Turns out no matter who you are, accountant or otherwise, everyone needs a little of my newfound attitude in their life! Saying 'Fuck it' doesn't mean you use the term dismissively to get out of things you don't enjoy (like going to the dentist or, in the world of accountants, trying to make figures reconcile!), and by no means does my encouragement of you to say 'Fuck it' more often mean accepting or encouraging mediocrity. Quite the opposite, in fact.

When you start saying 'Fuck off' to messages that are no longer serving you, you create a lot of space within your mind to dream again, and energy to channel elsewhere.

THIS IS WHAT I ALSO SOMETIMES REFER TO AS A

sparkle activity.

When I speak to audiences about injecting more sparkle into their lives, and give examples of what I mean by sparkle activities, the energy in the room changes. Whether I'm speaking to 100 people or 1000 people, there is a shift in the way the audience reacts to the notion of a sparklier life. People lean their bodies in, they shift ever so slightly to the front of their chairs and a few knowing smiles creep in and little glimmers of cheekiness appear in people's eyes.

It's a fundamental human desire to want to feel joy and happiness and yet so many people have allowed the 'b' word to get in their way of accessing these highly powerful and incredibly health-optimising feelings. I'm not referring to the word 'bitch' – although this 'b' word getting in the way of you living a sparklier existence certainly is one of those! – I'm talking about being busy. Busy! Busy! Busy! Have you noticed how quick we are to say how busy we are to anyone who asks? Being busy has reached pandemic proportions, or at least it seems to me, with so many responses to questions about our daily existence consisting of busy, busy, busy!

For so many people, due to living busy lives, the idea of engaging the part of themselves that likes to participate in happy, joyful activities is too difficult or time-consuming to imagine. Some people are so busy they're yet to realise they can say 'fuck off' to negative messages around them. Too many people are not engaging in sparkly activities. Well, eat glitter for breakfast and sparkle all day, I say!

Engaging in sparkly activities sounds childlike, and it's meant to. 'Sparkle activities' are things that fill you with joy and happiness, reconnect you with your younger self or your inner child that's screaming out for more fun and less complacency. If you can, right now, take a moment to reflect and recall the last time you had some hardcore, unadulterated fun? Fun, as in doing an activity that pushed you to feel scared or made you laugh so much you nearly wet your pants. Any activity that made you feel *alive*.

Unsure what constitutes unadulterated fun, or what equates to a 'sparkle activity'? Look at the list on the next page. Have you done any of these activities recently? If so, do you remember how you felt when you engaged in them?

Sparkle activities include, but aren't limited to:

- Skinny dipping
- Stand-up paddleboarding
- Doing a hip-hop class
- Learning to knit
- An all-body massage
- Reading a book in a forest
- Swimming in a lake
- Doing volunteer work
- Riding a camel
- Climbing a mountain
- Sleeping under the stars
- Going on a ghost tour
- Staying in bed all day to watch your favourite movies
- Having a picnic in the park
- Going on a swing
- Singing karaoke
- Paddling in a kayak
- Going to the movies on your own
- Riding a horse
- Going on a rollercoaster
- Dancing in your lounge room
- Getting a tattoo
- Going for a motorbike ride
- Dying your hair a different colour
- Doing basically any activity . . . naked!

It goes without saying that modern-day life is busy. I get it, I run a global organisation, have staff, have friends and kids, a dog and even a bloody turtle that the kids were meant to look after but of course don't! There are always demands on my time and people wanting something from me. And that's why it's even more important to take time out and schedule in sparkle activities. You can't be of service to others unless you look after yourself first and fill up your cup. It's such a cliché, but I am going to go there – put your own oxygen mask on first!

So why, if sparkle activities feel so good, don't we engage in them on a more regular basis? It's quite simple. Humans are inherently lazy. We are creatures of habit, and we don't naturally like to take risks, push ourselves or explore new territory. We like familiar surroundings and feeling secure and safe. It's for these reasons that we need to give ourselves a regular nudge to extend ourselves beyond our comfort zones, because as they say, that's where the magic happens.

THE MAGIC HAPPENS OUTSIDE OF *your comfort zone.*

A few years ago, when Nigel Marsh, co-founder of Earth Hour and founder of the Sydney Skinny, rang me to extend an invitation to participate in the Sydney Skinny, my initial thought was, 'Are you freaking serious?' There was no way in hell that I was going to get my kit off in front of hundreds of people before taking part in a nude ocean swim!

In terms of sparkle activities, this one is off the Richter scale. But then I asked myself some questions.

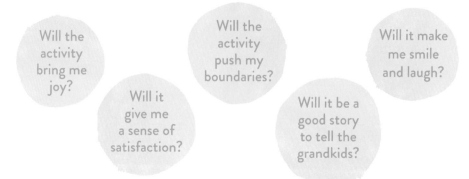

Will the activity bring me joy?

Will it give me a sense of satisfaction?

Will the activity push my boundaries?

Will it be a good story to tell the grandkids?

Will it make me smile and laugh?

The answer to all of the above was yes! This was a red-hot sparkly activity, and I just had to do it. Turns out the Sydney Skinny didn't disappoint. It now sits proudly on the Top 10 list of the best things I have ever done.

Nigel is one of my favourite people on the planet, and I'm grateful I call him a friend. If you've seen *Embrace*, you'll recognise these words from him that have a profound impact on viewers, staying with them long after screenings:

> People don't properly reflect on what's important to them, not because they're nasty, but because they're rushed. It takes one of the 'big four' before they properly reflect – death, divorce, disease, redundancy. We all know people who've had tragedy in their life and they go, 'You know what? I've had a think, and what's important are these things . . .' If they hadn't had those events in their life, they wouldn't have stopped and paused.

Well, I don't want to compare myself to the 'big four', but think of this book as your pause. Your opportunity to reflect.

The truth is, I've never met anyone who has engaged in a sparkle activity and has regretted their choice to do so. I tell a lie; sometimes when people engage in physical sparkly activities they've not done before they often use muscles that have lain dormant for years, so I do get the occasional angry text from someone who's a little sore (but with jest!). For the most part, doing an activity that brings joy, laughter and a sense of adventure into your life is always a good choice.

I think it's important to acknowledge that sparkle activities don't need to be big, loud or life-altering experiences. They can be small acts, like picking flowers on the walk home from school with your kids, so long as they lead you to feel positive and happy.

You've learnt to say 'Fuck off' to negative messages around you.
Now it's time to say 'Fuck it' and walk towards the light.

EMBRACE YOURSELF

Nigel Marsh

Founder of the Sydney Skinny and author of *Fat, Forty and Fired*, *Overworked and Underlaid* and *Fit, Fifty and Fired-Up*

I believe life expands or contracts in direct proportion to your courage, that the magic happens outside your comfort zone. But the trouble is for many of us, the passing of years results in our appetite for risk shrinking.

I know people who haven't taken a risk in over a year, people who can't even remember the last risk they took. Losing your sense of adventure, however, is no joke. Your sense of adventure is like a muscle – if you don't use it, it atrophies, which is a tragedy.

When I look back at my life, all the best decisions I've taken (asking my wife to marry me, having kids, moving countries, etc.) have involved significant risk. How sad, therefore, is it to stop taking risks? To basically settle for no more great outcomes in your life. To shrink in your experiences and impact in this life and on those you love.

This is one of the key reasons why I set up the *Sydney Skinny*. It is designed as a safe, joyous event to enable people to step outside their comfort zones and a small harmless way to get back in touch with their sense of adventure.

I've deliberately set the bar incredibly low – it's an all-ticketed event, held in a secluded national park, with no spectators. An event where you are clothed on land, naked only on the beach and under water – and when you come out of the water, you immediately get given a sarong to cover yourself.

Your internal response to the notion of doing the swim provides an incredibly important personal data point. If your response is basically, 'Oh my god, that's way too risky, I could never do it!' that's fine – forget my swim.

But just take a moment to check if this response is representative of your sense of adventure in other areas of your life – your social life, family life, sex life, career, whatever! Because if it is, I humbly and lovingly suggest you might just not be living life to the full. And that would be a crying shame.

WHAT SPARKLE ACTIVITIES WOULD YOU LIKE TO DO?

Over the next few months, can you commit to one sparkle activity
a month? Share your sparkle moments on social media so I can see!
Just hashtag #ihaveembraced

_____

_____

_____

_____

_____

_____

Let's talk about sex

Got YOUR ATTENTION, DIDN'T I?

If you're gorgeously naïve and think I'm referencing the lyrical sensation released by Salt-N-Pepa in the 1990s, you'd be mistaken. (If you don't know the classic, shame on you!) If you think I'm about to talk about sex, you're correct. So let's just lay down a few ground rules:

1. Mum, this chapter is not for you.
2. Dad, this chapter is not for you.
3. Mum and Dad, would you *really* expect anything less from me in a tell-all book? But seriously, go to the next chapter – both of you!

I would also like to acknowledge that I've met an alarming number of women who have experienced sexual abuse and assault, and who therefore have a complicated relationship with sex. If this is you, please know that you are not alone and that if this subject matter triggers you, in no way do I expect you to read further. I also strongly encourage you to seek support, if you haven't already, and professional help aimed at healing these wounds and loving yourself more.

If it crossed your mind to skip or skim read this chapter too, perhaps because the word sex makes you blush or the thought of an in-depth review of the *Kama Sutra* isn't really your thang, you'd be missing out. Why? Because helping you embrace and firmly grip that golden ticket simply wouldn't be complete without addressing the very act that brought you here!

Now, let's begin. I recently had the pleasure (platonic pleasure – mind out of the gutter!) of travelling to the incredible Australian outback to speak at an event put on by women, for women, who live in the bush. (Sheesh, stop giggling at the word 'bush' already!)

For those of you who have never been to the Australian outback, it's breathtakingly beautiful. I feel so lucky to have been born in this incredible country, and even luckier to have my body image activism be a way for me to experience equally powerful and peaceful places. One of the only downsides is that they call it the outback for a reason. I mean, it's seriously out the back – you can drive for hours and not see a single car pass by. For those who live there, it can be bloody lonely.

When I was invited to be keynote speaker at the annual Channel Country Ladies Day event in Jundah, Queensland, there was no way I was going to miss the opportunity to speak at such a memorable event. And when I say memorable, my gosh it was – and not for the reasons I thought it would be.

The first annual Channel Country Ladies Day took place five years ago. Started by two women who recognised the absence of opportunities for the ladies of remote Queensland, the event aims to reduce social isolation and increase emotional wellbeing. It's an event where women of all ages come together and enjoy an uplifting break from the demands of everyday life in the bush. It's a big event in the calendar of women across the region, and many new friendships are formed. The event also, in some cases, gives women their only access in the year to health and recreational services including massages and manicures!

Prior to attending, I imagined that women living in the bush must find it difficult to let off steam without the outlets that we city-folk take for granted. When I thought of people living in isolation, the city slicker in me twitched ever so slightly at the thought of not having a local yoga studio or gym to move my body in. The thought of not being able to browse shelves at the local shops or meet friends at a cafe or bar for a burger and a laugh was a very foreign concept for me.

When I thought about the event, and how these women would behave when they came together, I imagined it would be a pretty wild show, like a circus coming to town or a new kid joining the class mid-year. I imagined that the novelty of such a big event would unleash booze drinking like it was constantly happy hour, and that I'd see women doing the worm across the d-floor!

Yes, on the Friday night I did witness some pretty epic moves and fun times, but on the Saturday night I noticed the dance floor was a little less busy.

I overheard one of the event's committee members asking another where everyone had gone. After a short while, we noticed a market stall in the distance that was ten-people deep in women all vying for a peek at the wares for sale. As we walked over, I tried to imagine what goods they might be selling – what was appealing enough to clear a dance floor and be worth queuing for that long in the heat? Surely lavender soap and scented candles couldn't cause this much commotion . . .

As I moved closer, I saw a woman talking passionately with what looked like a kitchen utensil in her hand. 'Fuck me,' I thought to myself. 'A cooking utensil demonstration? It's Saturday night, for God's sake, people. And there's not a kid to look after in sight!'

'WE SHOULD BE OUT PARTYING AND *grinding to some R'n'B.'*

Grinding indeed. That was a vibrator in her hand!

Waving around a sleek – but might I add *giant* – vibrator, a fabulous woman by the name of Sally had brought a mobile sex shop to the middle of the desert. Like a messiah standing before a group of diehard parishioners, she was sharing the gospel of dildo with the women of the outback.

Rifling through luggage filled with vibrators, cock rings and other small devices I wouldn't know where to put, yet alone how to derive pleasure from, I couldn't believe what I was seeing.

Quick disclaimer. I need to make it clear to my newfound outback friends that I am in no way suggesting women of the bush are a horny breed. Instead, I acknowledge and praise your sense of adventure in curiously seeking out what, in my opinion, not enough women are.

Self-pleasure, otherwise known as masturbation, is still quite the taboo subject for women. While all the men I know in my life are encouraged to wank whenever they please as part of a healthy lifestyle (except my dad, of course, who I hope to God isn't still reading this), for women, the idea of openly talking about masturbation, other than referring to an episode of *Sex and the City*, is just plain 'dirty'.

Self-pleasure is an expected behaviour for men to engage in. Take porn, for example. You rarely see a woman orgasm and then hop off the man and leave him with a huge erection! Men are entitled – expected – to get their rocks off, and as Sally so rightly pointed out at her stall, this double standard between the sexes is so ingrained that many women aren't even aware of how our sexual organs function.

When a young boy touches his genitals, it's thought of as cute or normal, but when a young girl behaves with the same curiosity she's told 'don't touch'. Body-image conditioning starts young, and it's gender conditioning like this that leaves little wonder many of us have spent more of our lives punishing our bodies rather than loving and enjoying them.

During the outback event, there was a series of workshops being held by a variety of different leaders. There was a Brazilian dance workshop, an African drumming workshop and a financial planning workshop, to name just a few. Would it surprise you, based on the theme of this chapter, that a sex workshop was the first to meet its quota of participants? Method of entry was via your name added to an A4 sheet of paper, and let's just say the sheet ran out of lines!

I went along with great interest to the workshop, not so much for the education on sex toys (although hello, bonus!) but rather due to my fascination with how the women were going to interact with the subject matter. Sally was as nonchalant as one could be when explaining the

plethora of sex toys she'd brought with her, explaining the function of each, one by one.

Sitting three seats down from me was Ellen, a comedian who became my wing woman for the trip. Helping calm my nerves on the small chartered flight necessary to make it to the event, within twelve hours of knowing each other she'd rubbed my back and I'd shared numerous poo stories with her – a recipe for lifelong friendship. Sitting between Ellen and me were two women, one in her sixties and the other in her seventies. At the beginning of Sally's presentation, I could sense by the women's body language and general vibe that they were somewhat reserved. So when Sally pulled out some vibrators to pass around, I was dreading the thought of having to keep a straight face when someone my mother's age passed me a giant penis!

In the beginning, our exchange was as swift and seamless as an Olympic relay team, grabbing the vibrator with one hand and passing it with care to the other. As each vibrator was passed to me, I noticed the women's energy shifting from an elevated and heightened sense of awkwardness to that of ease, so much so that one proceeded to ask, 'Is this good for the clitoris?' Say what? Who are you and what have you done with the timid woman who was sitting next to me?

There were two clear highlights of the day for me. The first was when I turned to the woman sitting next to me and she was using a vibrator to massage her neck. The second was watching Ellen gently prod the woman next to her with a vibrator to help lighten the mood. And while this all sounds quite funny – and let me tell you, it was – there's a serious side to all this vibrator tomfoolery. The fact is, not enough women are turning to their bodies for pleasure. Women are not masturbating enough!

How do we move past the shame, guilt and embarrassment of self-pleasure and sexual enjoyment? To begin breaking down the barriers to masturbation, we need to collectively reimagine the experience and call it something that doesn't mortify or force mouths to drop in shock. Personally, I like the term coined a couple of years ago by a lady participating in a workshop I ran with my dear friend Dr Gemma Munro (a fabulous performance psychologist): Tinkerbelling.

Then, we need to celebrate all that Tinkerbelling does for us. I'm no expert, but here are just a few reasons to sing the praises of self-pleasure:

- Tinkerbelling forces us to be mindful and live in the present.
- Tinkerbelling supports our self-worth, and acknowledges that we are deserving of pleasurable experiences.
- Tinkerbelling releases the hormones dopamine and oxytocin, both widely accepted as positive mood lifters.
- Oh, and did I mention that Tinkerbelling is fun and free?

Finally, we need to do exactly what we did in the outback and what us women do best. We need to talk, we need to connect and we need to share our experiences. We need to create a safe space with our girlfriends to share and tell our stories – the good, the bad, the ugly and the awkward. Sharing our stories will empower us, allow us to learn from one another and, most importantly, give one another permission to let go of any feelings of shame, guilt or embarrassment.

(Mum, you dirty dog, I know you are still reading this! Something to talk about at our next girls' day? Dad, if you're still reading this, I can't even . . .)

I know for some of you reading this, having a conversation about masturbation with a friend might feel scary and just too much. So, I've collected the following from women within my circle to help you take the next step towards embracing sexual pleasure.

LET'S

celebrate

ALL THAT

Tinkerbelling

DOES FOR

us.

EMBRACE YOURSELF

'I'd been married for twenty-five years and I'd never masturbated. I didn't know how, and I didn't know my body. I heard about a woman in New York City who taught women how to do it: masturbate. It was one of the most confronting, vulnerable yet liberating experiences of my life. I stripped down bare in front of this stranger, opened my legs and learnt about my body through a small mirror. It was the best thing I ever did!'

Deena, 63

'When my husband died fifteen years ago, I was faced with the fear of never feeling good or having an orgasm again. I taught myself to look after myself. My grandkids wouldn't have a clue.'

Dorothy, 82

'Some people have an apple a day. I have an orgasm a day. People wonder how I operate at the level I do. Well, the secret's out!'

Hannah, 41

'I remember when I was at school camp as a teen, a friend in
my cabin asked the rest of us whether we had masturbated.
She was very matter-of-fact, in no way trying to be provocative or
funny, and at the time I was so embarrassed. I remember thinking
how odd she was to do such a thing and how she must have been
a bit of a slut! Looking back, I think, "Wow, how bloody wise you
were at such a young age to be so in touch with your body,
and so comfortable with self-care!" We're still
friends to this day, and she remains one of the
most body-confident people I know.'

Mic, 33

'I don't have an orgasm every time
I masturbate, but I do like the time I create
to have some intimacy on my own.
I take a bath, light a candle . . .
it's like having a mini-date
with myself. It's a weekly ritual –
it's my time.'

Katherine, 26

EMBRACE YOURSELF

Viva la vulva

'The VAGINAS MUST STAY!' I declared.

I'll never forget the day the *Embrace* documentary team and I sat around a boardroom table talking about the repercussions of including twenty still images of a beautifully diverse range of vulvas in our film.

'They'll never get through,' our editor said, shaking her head, to which the rest of the table agreed.

It was a risk to include them, that's for sure, but I was adamant that they stay despite the trouble those pesky vulvas might cause us. And trouble they caused us indeed.

Now, let's hold up. I'm not just using the world vulva over vagina because it sounds better. Just like learning that we women have three holes down there instead of two, I was shocked to learn that the terms vagina and vulva refer to completely different things.

Vulva is a term used to describe all the external bits we can see when staring head on (you get the gist) at a woman's genital region. The vulva encompasses the mons veneris (pubic mound), the labia majora and minora (the larger and smaller flaps) and the all-important clitoris, and serves to protect the urethra and (drum roll) . . . your vagina! Your vagina is the canal inside you that goes all the way up to your uterus, and is the slip'n'slide your baby will travel down should you ever experience childbirth.

In Australia, like other countries, we have a government body called the Classification Board that reviews film and television content prior to release. One of the Board's roles is to suggest a particular piece of content's appropriateness for different age groups. For instance, they use a rating system to help 'protect minors from seeing harmful content'. The rating system ranges from G (suitable for all ages) to R (only suitable for those over eighteen years of age). In between these ratings are PG (parental guidance recommended), M (for mature audiences) and MA15+ (for those over fifteen years of age).

We expected that *Embrace* would be rated M. We expected that the Board would believe, as we did, that the content requires a certain level of maturity to comprehend its message. An M rating would indicate to parents and educators that the film was in no way a walk down Sesame Street. However, if a child under fifteen years was mature enough to understand (or had been affected by) the global body-image epidemic, they should be able to see the film so long as an adult was present with them.

We were utterly devastated when we received the restricted rating of MA15+. Somehow *Embrace* had made its way into the same classification rating of *50 Shades of Grey* and Alfred Hitchcock's *Psycho*! What made it even worse was the response from the Classification Board as to 'why' they had chosen the rating: because part way through the film, multiple photographs of female genitalia are shown in a series of close-up images, some including 'protruding labia', while a woman discusses the different appearances of women's vaginas.

Hang on a second!

DID I JUST READ THAT CORRECTLY?

Did the Classification Board just body shame a documentary on positive body image? I was shocked – and outraged – and couldn't help myself from responding passionately, my fingers furiously hitting the keyboard.

> Dear Australian Classification Board,
>
> You made a terrible mistake when you gave our documentary *Embrace* a restricted rating of MA15+ because of a couple of (in context and educational) still images of women's labia. What shocked me the most was the reference you made in particular to 'protruding labia'. Shame on you for shaming women's bodies.
>
> If you think that we would be silenced by your unfair and unjust rating, how very wrong you are. As you may have seen, we've applied for a waiver to appeal the decision.
>
> I understand that if we don't get the waiver to appeal, it could cost the Body Image Movement in excess of $10 000. Well, I'm just giving you the heads up that I am not going away – nor are the women (and men) in the Body Image Movement community. We will raise the funds needed to appeal this decision, even if it means having a bake sale!
>
> Respectfully, Taryn

VIVA LA VULVA

Turns out that thanks to a small miracle, the bake sale wasn't necessary, with our application to waive the $10 000 appeal fee approved. And despite being told that the decision would never be overturned because the Board's decision was unanimous, I was ready to fight.

I was ready to fight for every woman who felt her body was abnormal because it didn't shape up to what is shown in porn films or magazines. I was ready to fight for every woman who has unnecessarily turned to the surgeon's knife to remove parts of her body out of shame. I was ready to fight for every child – including my daughter – who grows up in this world assuming societal embarrassment about a body part that births new life. I was ready to fight for what was right.

I turned to my community for support, and support they did. The first thing I did was launch a worldwide survey, asking people whether they thought including the vulva photos in the film was helpful in promoting a healthy body image. Within a few hours, the survey had received over 1000 exceptionally positive responses, with 98 per cent of participants expressing gratitude for the inclusion of the vulvas.

Other than in pornography, many of us haven't seen another woman's vulva. It's not the kind of conversation you have with your mates over a latte, now, is it? 'Mind dropping your daks, babe? I just want to see what your girlie parts look like.' And in terms of porn, in one of the rare opportunities we have to see another woman's naked body, we're overwhelmingly presented with vulvas that are 'neat', 'tidy' and predominantly hairless!

What is perhaps most disturbing about the lack of vulva representation is our perception of them – the belief that if ours doesn't look similar to what we've seen, we're not normal. This then creates shame, fear and immense embarrassment. In a recent survey of 443 Australian GPs, a third had seen patients aged under eighteen years who wanted to reshape their genitalia. Almost all of the doctors surveyed said they had seen women of all ages express concerns about the appearance of their genitals.

As I reflect on this now, the shame women and girls feel about their vulvas has caused a stream of tears to roll down my face. It breaks my

I WAS READY TO

fight for

every woman

WHO FELT

her body

WAS ABNORMAL.

EMBRACE YOURSELF

heart, not just because I am a mother of a young girl, but because I am a woman who understands that shame and embarrassment.

I vividly remember growing up thinking something was wrong with me. I'll never forget the first time I saw a women's vulva in a men's magazine in primary school. I was so young when my friends and I found the magazine, and I was so confused by its content. Nevertheless, I saw it.

'OKAY,' I THOUGHT TO MYSELF,

that's what it looks like down there.'

And so, when I got older, when mine didn't look like the only visual representation I'd ever seen, I became incredibly self-conscious. And many of my friends felt the same.

When I was about seventeen, after a few too many drinks, I was with my girlfriend in the bathroom. To cut a lengthy story short, I basically suggested that 'I'd show her mine if she'd show me hers'. I was desperately searching for acceptance and to feel normal, so when I took a peek (and she peeked at mine) a weight instantly lifted off my shoulders, and I think hers too. We kind of looked the same. We were 'normal' after all.

Speaking of normal, one of the most beautiful (yet heartbreaking) stories I've ever been told was at the Adelaide premiere screening of *Embrace*. A woman in her seventies came up to me with tears streaming down her face, just as mine are now writing this. I hugged her immediately, as I could sense she needed it, that she had experienced trauma. As I embraced her I thought, 'I bet she has a daughter who has an eating disorder.' But as it turned out, it was her own trauma that I was embracing.

She looked me in the eyes and said, 'Thank you for that film. For the first time in my entire life I feel normal.'

'Why?' I asked.

'Seeing the photos of the women's private parts was so liberating. I've always thought there was something wrong with me.'

The shame so many women feel about their bodies knows no bounds, from confused teenagers to self-conscious women in their seventies and everyone in between. Everyone is trying to work out if they are 'okay'.

VIVA LA VULVA

The response to *Embrace* and the vulvas by audiences across Australia was astounding. And amid trying to juggle the cinema release, Q&A screenings and a tonne of publicity, the classification battle was ongoing and about to go mainstream. The Australian media had picked up the story, and so #vulvagate began.

The funniest quote I read in relation to the #vulvagate frenzy was from friend Mia Freedman, co-founder and creative director of the Mamamia Women's Network media company. She said: 'More than 50 per cent of Australians have a vagina. The rest – I think it's fair to say – either came out of one, or go into one on a regular basis.'

True that, sister. True that!

As the discussion of vulvas spread from social media to mainstream TV and then newspapers at the height of the controversy, my dear and awesome mum decided to join Facebook. So randomly, among the chaos, Mum called me to ask, 'What's with all of this vulva business?'

I had to gently explain to Mum that it's not indicative of what I do every day. But her timing in joining Facebook – the day #vulvagate went viral – was impeccable!

After months of anxiously awaiting the Classification Board's decision, having been told the entire time that the important vulva scene was a classification deal-breaker, my wish came true. Serendipitously, on Mikaela's birthday, the *Embrace* rating went from a restricted MA15+ to an unrestricted M rating. Hooray for us! We'd won! The most exciting part of the decision was that *Embrace* would now be allowed to be shown in schools – to the younger generation that needed to see it most.

In other parts of the world, *Embrace* was much more, well, embraced!

In New Zealand, without any bother, the film was classified M. In the United Kingdom, there was no drama with the vulvas; instead, a few F-bombs needed to be deleted! Thank goodness that in the United States, international films don't require a rating (phew!) and, as for the Germans, it was *viva la vulva*!

Since making the film, vulvas (including my own) have been demystified to the point that I no longer bat an eye when seeing one. That is, unless you're sitting on a plane and *Embrace* comes on as part of the in-flight entertainment. Chicken, beef, vulva, anyone?

So, what can we all learn from #vulvagate?

Fight for what is right, even when you're told you won't win. Whether related to body image or otherwise, if there's an issue of injustice in life that you simply can't stomach, use your voice to amplify awareness. In turn, you will encourage others to use theirs.

Your vulva is powerful. Never forget it! It deserves your love and utmost kindness.

Vulvas come in many fabulous shapes, colours and sizes, and, just like our bodies, are equally beautiful and unique. Don't believe me? In my dreams, at this point I would ask you to 'lift the flap' (excuse the pun!) to reveal a page of vulvas. However, it was (reluctantly) agreed that perhaps the images were a little too risqué to print in this book, so if you would like to take a peep at a selection of fabulous and diverse photographs of women's vulvas, head to bodyimagemovement.com/vulva. Just make sure you come back to the book straight away and keep reading. Wink wink!

Jade Beall

Photographer and author of *The Bodies of Mothers:
A Beautiful Body Project* and *The Bodies of Mothers* and
*Photographing Motherhood: How to Document
the Lives of Women and Their Families*

This self-portrait is a diagram of how the world reminds me every single day how gross I am.

Menstrual blood is gross (but violent and gory movies are normal).

Cellulite is gross (most women have it, yet it's this dark secret few want to talk about and many would give their life to have removed).

Fat rolls are gross (but the bones on someone too thin are gross too).

Small breasts are gross (but surgery will fix me).

Pimples are gross (but antibiotics, which can cause skin cancer, are a good choice. How could I choose to offend other humans with my innocent pimples?).

Wrinkles and dark circles under my eyes are ugly (yet painful injections to erase away evidence of growing a privileged, long life happen at parties).

Confidence is sexy (but loving oneself is narcissistic).

It's no wonder so many of us struggle with depression – and think we are unworthy of feeling divine and sacred – when we've been ingrained to believe just how gross we are by simply being us:

women with beating
hearts and waves of
emotion and years
of living, crying, loving,
struggling, succeeding,
birthing, grieving
and ageing.

If I see you in a supermarket and you have stained the back of your white dress with menstrual blood, I will come and tell you how beautiful you are!

I am told that I am gross.

If I see your cellulite, I will compliment the beautiful aliveness of your skin and ask if you wanna see mine!

If I see your rolls or your bones, I will tell you how sacred, precious and divine your body is and how I wonder what it must feel like for your soul to breathe and dance in such a rad collection of molecules!

If I see your pimples, I will tell you that you are just like me.

If I see your wrinkles, I will tell you that you have lived a rich life.

Let's *love*, friends. Because, let me tell you – as someone who has watched her father take his last breaths in her arms – much too soon we have to say goodbye to these wild, funny, messy, fascinating, gorgeous, magical miracles we call bodies.

Bust a move

In ADELAIDE, WHERE I LIVE, there's a mountain called Mount Lofty
that lots of people run, walk and drag themselves up. It's really
challenging to get to the top, but it's a fun(ish) thing to do.

Over the years, with varying fitness levels, I've reached the top. I've
dragged myself up when my fitness was low, I've run the entire way when
I was super fit and, occasionally, when feeling positively overzealous, I do
things like piggyback my four-year-old daughter the entire way to the top!

You see, the thing about fitness and our health is that it's rare to
sustain a particular level forever. As humans we evolve, and so do our
levels of health and fitness, with some years feeling particularly packed
with energy and others going at more of a subdued pace. Sometimes life
is awesome; other times it's shit. Sometimes we are firing on all cylinders,
and some days we can barely lift our heads off the pillow.

Regardless of how fit or unfit we might be, shaming ourselves into
moving our bodies is not the *Embrace* way. Even if you have been more
sedentary than usual or eating foods that you perceive to be 'bad', moving
your body should never be a thing of punishment. Instead, it should be
a thing of pleasure.

Hiking up Mount Lofty with a human backpack didn't feel
particularly enjoyable at the time, but the reason I did so was to spend
time with my daughter and to achieve a sense of accomplishment when
I reached the top. If you know Mount Lofty, throw me a high five next time!

Never once did I set out on that epic adventure with the motivation of weight loss or building muscle mass. I did so because the activity filled my mind, body and soul with fulfilment.

WE NEED TO MOVE OUR BODIES BECAUSE

we love them,

NOT BECAUSE WE HATE THEM.

Do you know how many conversations I've had with friends who hate going to the gym, yet drag themselves there most days to do a class they don't actually like? It doesn't make sense. So many of us have boxed ourselves into thinking there is a right and a wrong way to move our bodies when really there's neither. Aside from performing a move correctly to avoid injury, there is no right or wrong way to move your body – only the right or wrong way to think about it!

The two most empowering steps I've taken towards regular exercise are changing the language I use to describe movement. I choose to partake in activities or movement, rather than 'exercise', which sounds punitive and gruelling. And I ask my body how it wants to move. Rather than creating rules for myself about how I should move my body, I listen to what my body feels it is capable – and excited – to do. If you set up rules around body movement (for example, 'I *must* go to the gym five mornings a week and do a spin class') there might be mornings you don't want to be around people or even get out of bed. Therefore, movement becomes a chore.

My old rules around exercise included the following:

- I must be dripping with sweat to call it exercise.
- I must exercise for a minimum of an hour.
- I must be puffed and exhausted.
- Exercise is hard, fast and loud. Exercise is not gentle,
  soft or quiet.

Sound familiar? The old me felt trapped by exercise. It was something that I 'had' to do. And not for the gains (a positive mind and improved health), but to lose weight and change how I looked.

The new me allows my body to decide if and how it wants to move. I've made the decision that I want to move my body every day because I know it makes me feel good, gives me more energy and provides mental clarity, but how I go about this changes as frequently as I change my underwear!

Some days I feel going for a gentle jog; other days I feel like lifting heavy weights. Some days I feel like thrashing around in a group fitness class, and on others I feel like walking barefoot at the beach. Occasionally I go to the gym, and sometimes I do get into a routine, but it's never a set objective – and there are no rules.

I've been on the endless transformation road that I imagine many of you are on now. I understand that constant desire to change your body for the 'better' – to make it thinner, hotter, lighter, curvier and more toned – and to be frank, it's exhausting! However, it doesn't have to be that way. If I was able to shift my mindset and move for pleasure over punishment, you can too!

So how do you make the shift? I implore you to take a li'l advice from Young MC's classic 'Bust a Move' and do just that – bust all the myths you have about physical activity or exercise and, instead, just move!

BUST A MOVE

EMBRACE YOURSELF

To begin, it's important to recognise that making any sort of change to the life you're living now is going to require some effort. It's important to recognise that your new attitudes towards movement come from an empowered place, and equally important to recognise that it may take time and mental energy to shift the way you view physical activity. Remembering these two things will help you on days when it's tough. Stay with me, though – the benefits of moving for pleasure instead of punishment will far outweigh the effort required to make that mental shift!

Changing the way you move your body is going to be particularly difficult when you hear ridiculous phrases like 'Summer bodies are made in winter'. Have you heard that one before? What a crock of absolute shit! Let it be known that bodies are made when sperm fertilises an egg – that's how a body is made!

Please remember that the weight loss, fashion, advertising and beauty industries are going to try and put the fear of God into you (coincidentally around the time their sales take a dive in winter), but don't believe the hype! Whatever the body-shape trend may be at any given time – whether it be big butts or small waists or toned legs – you are going to be told that your body isn't good enough and doesn't measure up. How else can they sell you their 'product' as a solution, if they haven't first made you feel inadequate?

On the flip side, if you do believe the hype and make a beeline for the gym and green smoothie bar, you'll be met with the message that only certain body shapes and sizes can be healthy. You just can't win! You work out consistently during the week, drink plenty of water and have a butt that's firmer than a ripe peach from squats and star jumps, but because you aren't 'skinny', your good health simply can't be acknowledged.

I think it's important to interject here by telling you this: ALL body shapes and sizes are capable (and worthy) of movement. And ALL body shapes and sizes are capable (and worthy) of being healthy.

Move your body FOR pleasure, NOT PUNISHMENT.

EMBRACE YOURSELF

When I think about my own weight, I must admit I can't help but consider the damage I've done to my body over the years. In particular, when I think about the fitness competition I entered for which I lost fifteen kilograms in fifteen weeks to fit 'perfectly' into a body builder's bikini. In those last few days I completely depleted and dehydrated my body and felt anything but healthy. The fallout of radical weight loss is huge, and yet so many clever and intelligent people I know throw themselves heart, body, mind and soul into this pointless ring of fire.

When I lost the weight, I was told I was 'inspirational'. I always found this hard to reconcile because I was gym-obsessed, I maniacally weighed my food and I was constantly grumpy from trying to fight my body's genetics. This was inspirational? I knew the people giving compliments were well meaning, but heck, it really messed with my brain to hear that weight loss was an extraordinary act of discipline and strength of character! When you learn that all forms of deliberate weight loss are a fight against your body's predisposition, you realise that those people trying to lose weight aren't in need of celebration – they're in need of education.

We have been programmed to strive for the happiness that ensues from wearing a dress size smaller than usual or seeing a lower figure on the scales when weighing yourself, but this gratification (the result of endless hours pumping iron or working up a sweat) are fleeting and temporary. Moving your body from a place of intuition, respect and empowerment, however, brings peace and happiness for a lifetime.

Some musings on moving for pleasure over punishment . . .

- I want you to know that even though I talk about moving my body for pleasure, sometimes 'going hard' or being pushed and being challenged by movement feels good! Sometimes I push myself so hard an observer would think it's some kind of cruel punishment that I'm inflicting on myself, but sometimes I need to sweat and exhaust myself, and it's okay for you to do so too.
- Sometimes I choose mental satisfaction over physical enjoyment. It sounds like a complete contradiction to the 'move for pleasure' notion, but just like carrying Mikaela up Mount Lofty on my back, sometimes enduring an activity you don't like in the present can fill you with immense satisfaction in the end. For me, I relinquish physical enjoyment for mental satisfaction when I choose to run. I actually don't enjoy running, but I *do* love the mental satisfaction that it brings for hours after, so it's a mini trade-off I'm prepared to make!
- While I've made a commitment to move my body every day, sometimes I can get myself in mini funks where I prioritise other aspects of my life over my body's need to move. I can go a week or two doing nothing at all, which isn't ideal because mentally I can feel the difference. I wish I could be consistent,

but if you're like me and find life gets in the way of trying to move your body daily, be kind to yourself and appreciate you can only do your best!

- Tuning in to your body is key to embracing, but don't let your body play tricks on you. I experience this when my alarm goes off early in the morning, reminding me that it's time to move. My body's first reaction is, 'NO! I'm *really* happy right here. You don't need to move this morning.' So how do you know if your body is genuinely asking for a break or whether it's simply enjoying the comfort of bed? I've made a pact with myself and that pesky alarm. When it goes off, I get out of bed, go to the loo, grab myself a glass of water and give myself a five-minute window to assess how I'm really feeling – but *only* once I'm up! If I still feel like going back to bed after five minutes, I do without guilt. I'm listening to my body. But guess what? It rarely happens. After the initial shock of hearing that alarm, I rarely go back to bed!

EMBRACE YOURSELF

Embrace fitness as
joyful movement.

Louise Green

Athlete, coach, fitness activist and author of *Big Fit Girl*.

My story is not unlike that of thousands of women who've felt like they weren't enough. I may differ in that I found a way out and have since made it my life's work to help other women ditch the harshness surrounding exercise and wellbeing. Through my story, I hope you find freedom, as I did, as I unpack why exercise should be about joyful movement and never about punishment.

For more than a decade I desperately tried to alter my body into a smaller version of myself. I tried every diet, joined every gym – only to go for two weeks solid, then quit. I weighed myself excessively, and hated my body and my inability to 'control' myself.

My relationship with exercise was punishing and all-or-nothing. If I ate something considered 'bad', I'd hatefully threaten myself with things like, 'Look out. You're going to get it in the gym this week.'

The sole purpose of exercise was a tool and tactic like debits and credits. The more I could purge out in caloric expenditure, the more I could put in with food. I was treating my body like a machine with no feelings or humanity, constantly calculating its allowances, deficits and malfunctions. It was extremely unhealthy and, not surprisingly, totally unsustainable.

About fifteen years ago, on yet another quest to lose weight, I joined a 5k running clinic. For years, I marvelled over the glossy covers of running magazines and compared, examined and dismantled the bodies on the covers.

> I concluded that if I took up running, I too would look like these long, lean, running phenoms.

With an irrefutable case of impostor syndrome and an upheaval of fear frothing from my mouth,

I attended the first run night. I stood outside the run club watching all the 'real runners' laughing and high-fiving one another. In my size-16 body, trying to look indifferent, I watched with a deep loneliness and longing to fit in.

At that moment, they called us into the club for introductions. I sat with my head down until a woman decked out in running gear stood before us and introduced herself as our run leader. Her name was Chris, and that night, Chris changed my life forever. She wasn't like anything I had yearned for on the covers of those magazines, not even close. She was big – she was a plus-size athlete.

Her body was very similar to my own, and as I sat in disbelief, I felt my fear retract and my hope erupt like fireworks because maybe, for once, I did belong.

For the next twelve weeks we trained side-by-side, and Chris took me to my first finish line. Throughout our training she never once mentioned caloric expenditure, diets, achieving a smaller body or the inevitable looming bikini season. Her position on training was to unearth the athlete that was already inside me. She taught me to strive towards my best physical performance in the body I had. From that day forth, my relationship with exercise began to change from one of punishment to one of joy, and from aesthetic outcomes to physical power and athletic achievement.

I soon learnt that having a smaller body was not a precursor to athleticism. My body love and acceptance flourished, and I became unstoppable. I began to participate in all kinds of running races, long-distance cycling events, triathlons and conditioning programs. My love for movement grew, along with my confidence and capacity for possibility.

I eventually left my successful career as a talent agent and became fully certified to pay forward the message of 'athleticism at every size and shape' to other women. I now coach women to embrace fitness as joyful movement, personal challenge, team camaraderie

If we can start to approach fitness for joyful movement, endorphin highs and victory, then we really have a stake in changing the fitness industry's landscape and business model, making it less about preying on our insecurities and more about living our most joyful lives.

and for the purpose of building physical power and inner confidence. Most of all, I accredit movement as a privilege of being healthy and alive. I no longer weigh myself or care about calories expended, and I eat like an athlete, in healthy abundance, not restriction.

Over the past ten years I've helped thousands of women change their thinking around health and fitness. None of this would have been possible if it weren't for Chris and her courage to be seen and lead our group in her bigger body. If one plus-size runner can change every corner of my life, I think that speaks to the power of representation.

If we have the courage to be seen and represent a new paradigm of health and fitness in all our diversity, sweating it out with the best of them, then we have a chance to influence women off the sidelines and invite them into the game.

We cannot be what we cannot see, and it's up to us to be the visual representation many of us crave, just like Chris was for me.

I hope you will join this 'joyful' movement. It could change your life, and the lives of many women, for good.

Good food, bad food

It TOOK ME THIRTY-EIGHT YEARS TO WORK OUT that I was an emotional eater. You know the saying 'Can't see the forest for the trees'? That was me.

I was at my first session with a new personal trainer, Kelly, who asked me to take a questionnaire on my eating habits.

Do you crave specific food? Yes.

Is it hard for you to stop eating sweet things, especially chocolate? Naturally.

Do you eat when you are stressed, angry or bored? Yes.

Do you eat when you are feeling down or flat to lift your mood? Absolutely.

Does being alone increase your appetite? Yep.

Does eating give you comfort when you are feeling lonely? Ah, yep.

Kelly (also an accredited dietitian versed in mindful eating) smiled gently at the questionnaire I returned, her head nodding slightly.

'So,' I asked cheekily, 'looks like I passed with flying colours, then! Do you think I'm an emotional eater?'

She nodded, and we both acknowledged what I'd been struggling with my entire life: yes, I am an emotional eater.

A light bulb went off in my head. For the two years it took me to make *Embrace*, I'd put on a lot of weight. I can't give you a number, because I don't weigh myself, but I knew because my clothes were a little snug. When I travel, I get lonely. I experience homesickness, and I work such long hours that food becomes a much-needed reward. All those nights in bed, just me and a room-service burger, had led me to become the heaviest I'd ever been.

I had always been a little envious of those who, when stressed, lost weight. As a first-time filmmaker, navigating a new world and travelling often, my stress sought comfort in the blanket of peace that comes with eating food. The more I got stressed, the more I'd eat and the more weight I'd put on. Similarly, when I was sick, I would eat. In fact, food was a former religion. I loved and worshipped it, but far from the respectful way I do now.

When I ate chocolate, I used to feel bad. When I chose a salad over a burger, I'd praise myself for being 'good'. 'Good' and 'bad' foods agitated praise and pride or guilt within me to my very core.

In terms of diets, I'd done them all. When I was in my twenties, I jokingly referred to myself and my friends as 'Weight Watchers whores'. Every week I hopped on the scales and prayed for at least a kilogram of weight loss. Point eight of a kilo was disappointing, but okay – anything else deserved punishment via restriction.

Prior to the weight loss and calorie apps that exist nowadays, I would carry around my little notebook that recorded all of my weight-loss information. On 'good' weeks, I'd refer to it as a form of inspiration to keep me going. On 'bad' weeks, I'd look at it as a way to brace myself for a calorie-controlled day or two ahead. Losing weight was inspirational, or so I thought at the time.

The approach I took to dieting in my thirties was far more aggressive. I was either trying to lose large amounts of weight, or at the very least the last five kilos, and was always on a diet. Cabbage diet, 5 + 2, Atkins, Low-Carb High-Protein – you name it, I did it. But here's the thing . . .

Diets don't work.

(SHOCK HORROR!)

I know I'm definitely not the first to tell you this. And no, I'm not saying this competitively – as some may do – to stop you from staying on your current track to weight loss because I don't want you to get thin. I'm telling you this because categorising food into those that are 'good' and 'bad' means that you will miss out on the freedom of eating for enjoyment.

Megan Jayne Crabbe

Body positive advocate and author of *Body Positive Power:
How to Stop Dieting, Make Peace with Your Body, and Live*

When I was a child, my favourite weekends were the ones when my mother would bake a cake. Standing beside her, eyes wide and tastebuds trembling, I'd watch her pour the batter into the tin, the scent of vanilla swimming through the air, and wait to be handed the pièce de résistance: the whisk. I'd unapologetically lick it clean for the next ten minutes, glowing with happiness.

That was when food was just food. Something to enjoy, to look forward to; something that brought comfort and fullness, and made my Sunday afternoons sweeter. That was before the guilt crept in. Before the fear arrived. Before I learnt that food wasn't just food at all: food had the power to make my body bigger or smaller, and once I realised *that* the whisk never tasted quite the same.

It only took me a handful of years in the world to believe that a smaller body was a better body, and my body was too much. Diet culture got to me young, teaching me lessons that I would carry throughout childhood and into my teenage years: thinner is always a good thing; losing weight is a woman's life purpose; beauty only looks one way and dieting is how you get there. And so the dieting began.

Cutting back on certain 'treats' turned into cutting out entire food groups. Cutting out food groups turned into cutting out meals. Cutting out meals turned into counting every calorie every minute of the day. Recalculating. Bargaining. Weighing and measuring my worth by whether I'd eaten little enough to set the hand on the scale lower by the morning. Before I knew it, my entire life revolved around those numbers. And no matter how low I got them, it was never low enough. But I didn't realise that until much later, when I was twenty-one.

Standing on my bathroom scales, at the end of yet another summer spent starving and sweating myself smaller, I looked down and saw the number that was finally going to make me happy. The goal weight. I'd counted, I'd sacrificed, I'd turned food into the enemy and reached the Holy Grail of dietland. And I couldn't understand, after so many years of believing the lessons I'd learnt in my childhood, how I could still be so unhappy with my body. For the first time I wondered whether those lessons were true at all.

Why would the world teach women that shrinking their bodies should be their ultimate goal in life, when we're capable of so much more? Why do people believe in the power of diets to bring them happiness, when time and time again all we're left with is hunger and obsession? Why do we turn food into an enemy to be feared, and our bodies into battlegrounds to be conquered? Why can't we see that we've been lied to from the start?

The problem isn't food or our bodies. It's how we've been taught to see them. The biggest industries in the world make billions from teaching us to see our bodies as flawed, and selling us the solution. Our belief that our bodies are wrong is rooted in the fact that, 100 years ago, advertisers realised that turning female bodies into problems to be fixed could make them rich. Every diet plan, every pill, potion, wrap, detox, gadget and magic product promising happiness through that Holy-Grail goal weight can be traced back to a diet-industry profiteer with dollar signs in

their eyes. When I realised I'd spent a lifetime hating myself for someone else's bottom line, I was angry enough to refuse to buy into the lies any more.

Unlearning these lessons looked like throwing away my scales. It looked like quitting my diet group and promising to never go back. It looked like searching for beauty in bodies that I'd always been told didn't have any, and realising that they were overflowing with it. It looked like vowing to never count calories again, and learning to eat intuitively instead. It looked like letting go of fifteen years of fear, and making peace with food.

Eventually, it looked like licking the whisk clean without any of the guilt that I had held onto for so long. There I was once again, glowing with happiness. Glowing with the feeling of being free.

I FIRST HAD THE PLEASURE of meeting Dr Linda Bacon when I interviewed her for *Embrace*. Linda is an expert in the field of dieting and body physiology (and I'm not going to lie, the irony of having 'bacon' in her name wasn't lost on me!).

In a college in San Francisco, I sat and listened to her three-hour lecture, completely enthralled and intrigued by her words, her manner, her disposition and her depth of knowledge. I'm sure you'll see from her words of wisdom just why she's so inspiring.

Here are the ways in which I approach food these days, thanks to people like Linda:

- I eat to nourish my body so I have lots of energy.
- I respect my body, and know that eating food as close to nature as possible makes me feel good.
- I'm aware that diabetes is in my family, and I have a predisposition to the disease, so it's with this knowledge that I'm mindful of how much sugar I consume.
- I do my best to eat as mindfully as I can, which means I restrict eating in front of the television to occasional nights of the week.
- I do my best to listen to my body and when it has had enough to eat.
- When I overeat foods on occasion, such as a rare binge on chocolate or chips, I give myself kindness, not a guilt trip. The very next meal, I go back to my healthy and happy relationship with food.
- I no longer participate in diets or transformation programs.
- I don't weigh food, or myself.
- I no longer frantically obsess over food labels and calories. Rather, I focus on their ingredients.

- I believe that food is fun and joyous.
- If I feel like the cake, I eat the cake!
- I believe I know better than anyone on this earth what my body needs to thrive and flourish.
- I'm appreciative of my own amazing internal guidance system – my intuition!
- I feel a sense of gratitude towards food.

Diets don't work. I'm not sure why it took most of my lifetime to figure that out. In fact, I'm still unsure why highly intelligent women the world over continue to jump on and off the diet treadmill. It's been proven that 95 per cent of diets don't work, and yet we hold onto the notion that a successful diet (and subsequent weight loss) is going to make us happy.

When I stopped dieting and instead adopted principles of intuitive eating, I'd never felt more free. Learning to eat foods that nourished my body and gave me energy brought me a strong sense of empowerment, vitality and wellbeing – it was such a game changer.

A lot of the principles I adopted intuitively over the years, but some I adopted from Linda's revolutionary book *Health At Every Size*. It's one of the most fascinating and life-altering books I've ever read, and has had a profound impact on me and the lives of many in the *Embrace* community.

I am quite a spiritual person (I'm a big believer in signs) and perhaps the strongest evidence to embrace a life free from dieting lies in the word itself. Diet is a four-letter word, with the first three letters spelling 'die'. Would *you* engage in any other behaviour that spells out death to you?

I don't think so!

Dr Linda Bacon

PhD Researcher and author of
Body Respect and *Health at Every Size*

Diets. Don't. Work.

And here's the irony – dieting has probably contributed to why we're fatter these days than ever before. While 'experts' – and the presumption of common sense – have always touted diets as an antidote to high weight, the data shows otherwise. In fact, dieting is a well-established predictor of weight gain, as has been shown repeatedly in research.

Biology explains why few people sustain weight loss from a calorie-reduction diet. Scientists have identified many physiologic pathways that get activated to ensure weight stability. Our bodies have a system for managing our weight – which can compensate for our actions. For example, dieting triggers a reduction in the hormone leptin, which actually increases appetite and decreases metabolism – just the opposite of what you're shooting for if you're trying to lose weight!

And chronic dieting, well, that results in chronically reduced leptin release, which contributes to the well-established finding that the majority of people with a history of dieting gain weight over time.

Just check out what happened to the contestants on reality-TV show *The Biggest Loser* – six years after their hyped weight loss, a study of some of the contestants showed that the majority had regained most of the weight – and their metabolism had slowed dramatically. In other words, there were changes in their brain circuitry, which meant that eating less now resulted in weight gain. It wasn't the Biggest Losers' diet technique that led to this result; extensive research demonstrates that the same process occurs anytime body fat stores are reduced, regardless of method.

If you've ever dieted, think about your own experience. You reduced your calories and maybe also started or amped up your exercise. Doesn't matter whether it's low-carb, low-fat or low-sugar, the beginning stages can be pretty heady as you watch the scale needle drop. But then it gets harder to maintain. You probably found yourself thinking about food all the time. You started to feel desperate, and foods that never appealed to you before were suddenly calling out.

What the diet plans don't tell you is that biology lies behind that drive to break your diet. Your body's physiologic mechanisms underpin every one of the symptoms you felt. Even your tastebuds are affected when you diet, with the hormone leptin inspiring a process that makes a wider range of foods appealing. Biology can be powerful, and no matter how much willpower you think you have, it may be no match for the biological mechanisms triggered by your diet.

So, don't blame yourself if you give in and go off your diet. You're not a glutton or a weakling. In fact, most dieters show extraordinary self-restraint, persistence and determination. You didn't fail; the diet did. Maybe you had great willpower and resisted succumbing to the diet-breaking binge, and were able to 'just say no' despite the hunger. Some people even find that, after a while, the hunger signals dissipate and dieting gets easy. There is physiology behind that too: the body turns off those appetite signals rather than waste energy that it's trying to conserve, since you're ignoring the signals anyway. But that doesn't mean you lose weight. To compensate, your body could slow your metabolism, resulting in fewer calories burned. This explains why some people actually gain weight in response to cutting those calories.

Bottom line: Diets. Don't. Work.

This simple clarification can save you from a future of weight struggles, wasted time, energy and money, and feeling like a failure. Repeat after me: 'The diet failed, not me.'

This is good news: it shows your body is enormously powerful and successful at managing your weight. So, don't fight it: revel in it. You can relax about eating and enjoy your food. Let your body do what it does best. Trust yourself, pay attention to helpful signals like hunger and fullness, and everything's going to be okay. *The best way to win the war against fat is to give up the fight.* Let your body guide you to a weight that's right for you.

This isn't about giving up. All you're giving up is an ineffective way to get what you're really looking for. It's about moving on. It's about body respect and body trust, not body shame. It's what helps you make better choices about what to eat and how to eat, and other self-care.

Judgey pants

At ONE OF THE Q&A SCREENINGS OF *EMBRACE* IN AUSTRALIA, I was confronted head on with a lady who I'll diplomatically say was a little bit angry. The catty teenager in me would like to call her something else, but I'm a grown-up author now and should be more mature in my articulation. Who am I kidding? She was being a bitch.

I should preface this by saying that I'm the first to welcome feedback. In fact, criticism can be a really powerful driving force towards change. However, when comments thrown my way aren't constructive, I draw the line on my compassion and become a den mother protecting her lion cub – that lion cub being me!

The Q&A was going really well, with lots of intelligent questions raised by enthusiastic people who'd just seen the film. All of a sudden, this lady shouted at me from the middle of the audience in response to choices I had made in the film about my own body.

'How can we possibly listen to anything you have to say about embracing our bodies when you dye your hair and wax your legs? You *don't* embrace.'

The mood of the audience shifted from being positive and light to thick with tension. The room was full of supportive sisters ready to rip out 'Oh no you di-n't'. I knew better than to inflame the situation, but I couldn't resist, and proceeded to try to ease the awkwardness with a joke.

'My goodness,' I said. 'I feel as though I'm at a Trump rally!'

It only fuelled the fire. With that, Miss Thang stormed towards the stage in such a furious manner that I assumed a karate stance while waiting for security to come and save me. I secretly hoped I had the opportunity to air my perfected martial arts kata, but as we all know, words are what I'm famous for – not my fists.

'Okay, I got this,' I said, as I collected my thoughts (and the audience collected theirs). 'Let me put it like this. *Embrace* is about one thing – learning to love and embrace your body. Yes, *your* body. And when it comes to mine, only *I* will decide what I want to do to it.' I began to get my groove on, with the audience smiling and nodding their heads in agreement like the ultimate Taylor-Swift girl squad. 'If I want to dye my hair blonde because I have since I was seventeen, and it's habitual and it makes me happy to be blonde, I will.'

Yeah!

'If I want to paint my dial with pretty make-up colours one day and go bare-faced the next, I will.'

Fuck yeah!

'If I want to shave my legs, I will. If I want to grow my underarm hair, I will. At every stage, at any age, I will continue to make empowered choices *for me*.'

My body, my choices.

Your body, your choices!

EMBRACE YOURSELF

Cheers began to erupt in the room.

'There is no room in this Body Image Movement for people to judge anyone else for the decisions they make about their body. My body, my choices. Your body, your choices!'

This woman looked far from satisfied with my response, but had at least calmed the farm enough that she no longer looked ready to split my lip or pop me in the face with a right hook.

Later that evening, in the safety of my hotel room, I reflected on her behaviour and angst, but most of all, her judgement. I began questioning why she felt entitled to judge me, despite only knowing me from afar. And then I remembered. Oh, dear. If judging someone on face value was a crime, I'd be guilty as charged.

In the days when I hated my body, I judged others too. Too often. One day at the gym, I remember arriving for my usual high-intensity aerobics class (Olivia Newton-John, eat your heart out) to find that a new instructor was taking the class. I judged her immediately for how 'big' she was, about three dress sizes bigger than me. How could I possibly be inspired to give it my all by someone who didn't look after herself? I feel embarrassed now as I reflect on this thought – disgusted, in fact. However, my reaction had nothing to do with the instructor (who, I might add, had more energy and bounce than an Energizer bunny). My reaction came from a place of personal dissatisfaction.

You see, when you hate your own body, it's so easy to hate others. Spending the majority of your time hating on your weight, the size of your thighs and the perkiness of your breasts makes it feel almost normal to similarly judge those features in others.

Evolving from cavepeople who were constantly on edge, fearing the need to fight a mammoth for their next meal, our brains are designed to naturally scan environments for signs of threat. We have a tendency to focus on and give more weight to negative experiences and information instead of positive ones. This 'negativity bias' keeps us locked into a toxic pattern of behaviour that I'm calling bullshit on. Bullshit!

A scientifically proven behavioural pattern? Yes. A pattern of behaviour we need to continue adopting? No.

HOW CAN WE BEGIN TO JUDGE LESS AND

learn to love more?

Look for the positive. Just because our brains scan for the negative, it doesn't mean we can't actively participate in looking for the positive. Practising gratitude is one of the most helpful ways I've learnt to shift my mood from negative to positive in a matter of seconds. Give it a try! Think about something in your life that fills your heart with gratitude and joy. This thought will act as a magnet to continue attracting thoughts on a similar positive wavelength! This takes practice, but when we look for it, we can almost always find something positive about everything, and everyone.

Be empathetic. A friend of mine told me the story of how she was driving her car when she found out her dad had been taken to hospital, and that he was about to die. A few minutes later, she found herself sitting at the traffic lights on the wrong side of the road. She had no idea how she got there. A lot of people reacted with rage and anger, but in that moment she needed help, kindness and empathy.

What can we learn from this? Be quick to love, not to judge. Unless you're a mind-reader of telepathic genius, which I'm not, it's impossible to know what someone else may be going through.

Also, mind your own business! If you're a parent, like me, I'm sure you've either been part of or heard about another mother who is constantly on her phone while at the playground with her children. How 'un-present' of her. Doesn't she know she won't get that time back?

I wish I could package this more philosophically but I'll say it again: mind your own business. We don't know what this woman's story is, other than she's holding a phone to her ear and that she brought kids to a park. If she was chatting to her oncologist about how to manage chemotherapy side effects, I'd say it's a fucking triumph that she even *made* it to the park. You. Just. Don't. Know! Whatever someone's reasons are for looking, being or acting the way they are, we have no right to judge.

Embrace our differences. When other people's values don't align with ours, it's easy to judge them and their choices. But can you imagine how terribly boring life would be if we were all the same? When I was younger, I used to judge people who walked around wearing no shoes.

'Damn hippies,' I used to think. 'Bet they haven't showered in days – get a job!' Now I look at people who wear no shoes and think, 'Hey, nice work getting grounded.' Gone is my venom, gone is my nastiness and gone is my judgement. It's this kind of embracing that's become the foundation and strength of the Body Image Movement. There's plenty of room on this planet for all of us, and what's more, for our uniqueness.

A day or two after the *Embrace* Q&A, I got to thinking about that woman I was close to sparring with, and what might have brought her to the event in the first place. She may have come with a friend, unaware of what the film was about. She may have come with a daughter, hoping to shift her current desire to lose weight. Or perhaps, as I imagined, she came to see the film because she didn't love the skin she was in. Quite frankly, if she loathed her body as much I once did, her outburst was far less impassioned than what I may have let out!

ONE THING WAS FOR CERTAIN –

who was I to judge?

Jess Smith

2017 *Cosmopolitan* Woman of the Year,
former Australian Paralympian, motivational speaker,
founder of Join The Revolution and author of
Little Miss Jessica Goes To School

Despite our best efforts, most people make judgements as an immediate response to meeting or seeing a person for the first time. And when we make immediate judgements, it's often appearance-based. Although we know we shouldn't do it, judgement is something that is ingrained in so many of us.

> We grow up learning to be critical before we are accepting. Everyone has a story, and that story cannot be told or understood simply by looking at someone.

I've spent my entire life trying to navigate society and its assumptions of me based on opinions formed about my appearance. I was born missing my left arm, and then at just eighteen months old I suffered horrific third-degree burns to 15 per cent of my body after a hot water accident in the kitchen.

I know what it's like to look and feel different. Society was quick to label me: disabled, amputee, scarred; the list goes on. All of these words have negative connotations and undertones that I have spent years trying to disprove, and for a long time I was incredibly self-conscious and sensitive about my disability and prominent scars. Knowing that my body didn't fit the social standards of physical ability, it left me feeling inadequate and ashamed.

It's up to us to create change.

I desperately searched for ways in which I could push societal boundaries. Even though my self-esteem was almost non-existent, I managed to maintain an innate ability I had to prove people wrong. I've been able to use my body to demonstrate that I don't need to be limited by my physical appearance. Sport became my sanctuary, in particular swimming.

I rose to the top very quickly and at just thirteen was a rising star on the Australian swimming team. I represented Australia for seven years, travelling the world, winning medals and breaking records.

But success in the pool only masked my insecurities, which continued to develop dangerously. It wasn't as easy as swimming away from my problems.

By age fifteen my dwindling self-esteem morphed into an eating disorder. It started with dieting and skipping meals, and ended in bulimia and anorexia. I convinced myself that if I could obtain the perfect body – if I could control the controllable – surely people and society would look at me differently. Surely they would see past my obvious imperfections, and then I would feel accepted.

I like to believe that my courage, relentless application and natural aptitude enabled me to reach the Paralympics, at a time when my body was ill prepared both physically and mentally.

My experience didn't reach the Hollywood-movie ending, though. My Paralympic experience was overshadowed with disappointing results in the water, followed by more turbulence. This culminated in six weeks' hospitalisation, brought on by my eating disorders, which all but ended my international swimming career.

Years later, life is very different. I survived the ravages to emerge more resolute and self-assured than ever, becoming an advocate for positive body image. My recovery journey highlighted my need to be a powerful voice for others struggling with similar thoughts and feelings. With the support of family and professionals, I've now transformed into a motivational speaker and an avid campaigner, raising awareness of positive body image through social media platforms with the Join The Revolution campaign. I share my story with women and men of all ages, offering a personal and genuine perspective on eating disorders and body image.

After years embedded in this industry, I was amazed at the lack of real change that was being made. I was having the same conversations about negative body image over and over again. It seemed that everyone I met not only judged others, but they judged themselves: a vicious cycle of negative assumptions and dialogue that was contributing to a global epidemic.

I realised that I needed to start targeting a much younger audience. I wanted to prevent negative body image issues from even arising in the first place. But how could I talk to young children about body image issues in a way that would empower them?

I decided to write a children's book that challenged issues about disability, diversity and acceptance.

Judgement is something that starts at a young age. As a parent, I believe adults have an incredible responsibility to be positive role models and to show children and younger generations through our own actions and behaviour that everyone deserves to be appreciated for who they are, rather than how they look.

Body image is how we think and feel about our appearance. It's far more complex than many of us appreciate.

It encompasses race, ethnicity, gender, religion, culture, sexuality, mental health and the overall wellbeing of an individual. Moving forward, I want our collective focus on body image to no longer be about beauty and aesthetics, but rather a positive understanding of diversity.

When we judge another person, we allow ourselves to be judged. It's up to us to create change.

The Muppets, Lorna Jane and me

In 2016, WHEN *EMBRACE* WAS RELEASED in cinemas across the United States, my family and I spent five weeks there attending screenings, holding Q&As and pounding the pavement on publicity rounds. Taking the family to Los Angeles for such a long time was going to require some serious logistical planning, so I was beyond grateful when a woman I admire deeply – Emma Isaacs, founder and Global CEO of Business Chicks – reached out to me and offered a helping hand.

At this point, I'd never met Emma face to face. However, we knew of each other through various circles in Australia. Being the gorgeous woman she is, she and her equally generous husband, Rowan, offered for us (me, Mat, three kids and a heaven-sent nanny) to come and stay with them until we found our feet. While to some it may have seemed strange to stay with someone you've never met, but when the CEO of Business Chicks opens her doors to you, there's only one way to respond – with a resounding 'yes'!

I'd admired Emma for such a long time, so along with beginning the *Embrace* tour, I was thoroughly excited to arrive at LAX knowing the Brumfitts were about to finally meet the Isaacs. The thought of lying by the pool with Emma, sipping pina coladas as we mapped out our game plan for global domination, was dampened (albeit slightly) by the epic twenty-hour travel adventure that ensued. (This included Mikaela's tooth falling out mid-flight and needing to alleviate concern about the

Tooth Fairy's whereabouts.) Nevertheless, when we stepped off the plane, I was pumped, to say the least!

LA is just as colourful and full of celebrity as every Australian has been brought up to imagine. We were invited to screen *Embrace* at the Henson Studios where *The Muppets* was made – and, more exciting still, a bunch of Brumfitt guests and members of the Henson team gathered to watch *Embrace* in the quaint screening room of none other than Charlie Chaplin. I never imagined as a child I'd have a career that would allow me to name-drop Miss Piggy and friends, and the world's greatest silent film actor in the one sentence. But there I was, lapping it up.

Sharing Emma's generosity towards my family, and my admiration of her, with you is a way for me to show you how strongly I believe that there is plenty of space in this world for more than one woman with a powerful message to deliver. As if women need to be pitted against one another, fighting it out for supremacy of the social-change air space!

But there have been occasions when the media has tried to portray things differently. In one now-infamous example, I reached out to fellow Australian businesswoman Lorna Jane, and the media put a spin on things that got out of control. Through social media, I'd seen that she was in LA at the same time I was, so I invited her along to a screening of *Embrace*. Such a highlight of that particular tour was seeing Emma and Lorna, two incredibly dynamic women, enjoying the film, side by side. As soon as the credits rolled, Lorna turned to me and said, 'It really makes you think about things.'

I could tell by the tenderness with which she expressed herself that she was deeply moved by the film, and while on a Kermit the Frog high (metaphorical, obviously) I shared a photograph of the three of us on social media with the following caption:

I love dynamic, strong and unstoppable women, so it should come as no surprise that I love and adore these two – Emma Isaacs and Lorna Jane. We just had the pleasure of watching Embrace *at the Jim Henson studios – in Charlie Chaplin's old screening room – and it totally gave me goosebumps!*

Boy, did that late-night post on social media cause a stir – and a complex one at that! I never imagined, lying there in bed and sharing a quick post at the end of my day, that it would become headline news. So many of the people in my online community were furious with my choice to share the photo.

'Sorry, Taryn, I'm usually in full support of you and your mission. But standing there with Lorna Jane seems a little hypocritical,' said one woman.

'Lorna Jane is the poster girl for size snobbery – one movie and a photo doesn't change that!' said another.

Then this: 'I find it very disappointing that *Embrace* (and the Body Image Movement), who I have always seen as a strong voice for all women, would even contemplate acknowledging Lorna Jane as a woman who "embraces". She most certainly does not in any way embrace real women. Her whole brand, in every respect, defines women by size – and only tiny sizes!'

Oh, and this: 'WTF? Feeling very disappointed. Lorna Jane is more than likely "jumping on the bandwagon" to make a dollar here. Thank God most women are seeing through this stunt. Come on, Taryn, don't let us down.'

I've become accustomed to receiving negative comments from online trolls. Ever since I was first thrown into the public eye (when my 'before and after' shot went viral), I started to receive feedback from those I call 'muppets' – people who hide behind a keyboard much like a hand hiding inside a puppet. For the first time in quite a while, however, these comments about the photo with Lorna Jane actually hurt.

Being true to my word
IS A VALUE I HOLD DEAR.

The thought of disappointing people by going against what I preach fills me with immense anxiety. The worst thing I could ever do is let someone down, especially those in the Body Image Movement community, who I care so much about.

I was hurt, but also angry. Particularly angry when the media caught on to the matter faster than a pimple breaking out during your menstrual cycle. I responded with the following Facebook statement:

My DECISIONS ARE *always* GUIDED BY *intuition.*

THE MUPPETS, LORNA JANE AND ME

EMBRACE YOURSELF

I've just woken up (in a different time zone) so I've only just had the opportunity to read the comments about my recent Lorna Jane post.

It has long been my intention to get the film in front of Lorna and many other retailers around the world who *need* to see it. Therefore, the screening last night is a victory for the Body Image Movement, and for women around the world.

I'm proud to have such an active and vocal community who share their passion and thoughts. Who else needs to see *Embrace*? Which other retailers, organisations or individuals? At the Body Image Movement, we are dedicated to creating global change and we will use love and friendship to ensure our message is heard and shared.

I can understand, given the negative media publicity that Lorna has received over the years, why you might be angered and confused at my decision to invite her to a screening of *Embrace*. My goal was to connect with Lorna, to open up a conversation about how women are feeling, and to discuss what I think needs to be done to overcome the body-shaming and body-loathing epidemic.

After watching *Embrace*, I asked Lorna what she thought of the film and she said, 'It really makes you think about things'. Bingo! That is what *Embrace* does! It challenges people's beliefs and values. It challenges the way you think about diets and obesity. It challenges the way we stereotype people and the way we judge people. Most importantly, it encourages a new and positive conversation.

I would be an ineffective leader if I just comfortably positioned myself and my views in the safety of my community. We could spend the next fifty years talking amongst ourselves about positive body image and our dissatisfaction with the current lack of diversity in retail shops, advertising and the media. Do you know what the result would be – nothing! Nothing will change. The only way we can create meaningful change is to challenge the status quo, to encourage those people with different views to come and see another perspective.

Here are some of my other musings:

I believe you can like and connect with a person, even if you don't like or agree with every aspect of them as a person (or their opinions).

I don't believe (and nor should anyone) that the stories in the media are always true.

I respect that every person in business has the right to choose how they run their business and what they sell in their business.

I believe that sharing different opinions and opening up new conversations that challenge our beliefs and values helps to expand and cultivate change.

I'm sorry if I've disappointed some of you, but please know this: every decision I make is always with this community in the forefront of my mind. I've always acted with integrity, transparency and, mostly, passion. My decisions are always guided by intuition.

Intuitively, I believe that by expanding the conversation to a wider and broader audience, and by embracing all people (even those with opinions we might disagree with), we take an important step towards fostering acceptance and creating positive global change.

Taryn x

Lorna, equally unimpressed by the incorrect portrayal of our shared screening experience, expressed her wholehearted support of the Body Image Movement and me, and the inspiring work being done to encourage

women to embrace their bodies. She expressed the message in a way that aligned with her personal philosophy – and brand – and said how important it was to come together to support, inspire and love one another.

Following my statement and Lorna's, support and kindness flooded in from my community online and, surprisingly, the odd media outlet. This was a personal fave:

> *Thanks to Taryn Brumfitt, Lorna Jane might be looking to introduce a larger size range.* – Mamamia

Even more satisfying was that, shortly after we both responded to the outcry, the Lorna Jane brand used its first 'plus-sized' model in an advertising campaign.

For some, it may have been an insignificant move or perhaps a little too late to rectify the reputation of the brand. For others, it may have appeared to be an exercise in positive publicity. However, I like to think that it was the message of *Embrace* that facilitated the change. I can't predict the future of the brand, but I expect that more great things are to come – not only from Lorna and her team, but for other people and brands out there navigating the demand for diversity and representation.

Rules are for breaking

I WAS IN CALIFORNIA RECENTLY for some meetings, and found myself in a very unique situation. I had an entire Sunday to myself with nothing in the diary. Not a single soccer game to drive my sons to, or a party or play date to chauffeur my daughter to. While I love doing those things with my family on a Sunday, I adore one thing a little more – doing absolutely nothing!

I started the day with a yoga class at Wanderlust in Hollywood. It was my first time there, but my concern over being around people with their heads up their arses quickly dissipated when the welcome sign at the entrance was boldly emblazoned with 'Your ego is not your amigo'. Classic!

After yoga, I leisurely ate some avocado on toast and drank a mango smoothie (so virtuously LA, and so delicious), before blissing out at the beach like a 1990s school kid with not a care in the world other than catching that week's *Beverly Hills 90210*.

From there, I headed to Santa Monica where I walked around for hours. Stopping to rest my tired legs, a street performer caught my attention. He was playing some kind of musical instrument that resembled a recorder and sounded amazing, but he soon lost my attention as someone else entered my gaze.

I noticed a woman, perhaps in her late seventies or early eighties, with gorgeous Asian skin and a bun high atop her head. She wasn't part of his act, but she was dancing behind him, completely lost in his glorious music, dancing gently from side to side with her eyes closed and a slight smile on her face. She was dancing on her own, completely present and filled with enjoyment. I watched her in admiration, and it was in that moment that I found my spirit animal!

After half an hour of sitting and watching her dance, I noticed how people were beginning to laugh at her. Mocking her and teasing her. One man – around fifty years old – started to imitate her moves and turn to his buddies for approval of his joke. Of course, they bloody laughed too (the damn idiots). I became so fascinated by the appalling behaviour taking place that I ended up staying for an hour to watch.

The lens through which I looked at this woman was entirely different from those of the other people who passed her. I loved that she had a desire to dance, and, what's more, she just did it. She wasn't dancing to seek out the attention of anyone – she danced because that's what her soul begged her to do. It wanted her to move, to enjoy, to feel and get lost in the moment. She didn't give two fucks what anyone else thought of her, despite the majority of passers-by assuming she was crazy. But she was the least crazy person I came across that day. Want to know why?

Crazy is *not* moving your body when you want to, just because of what someone else might think. Crazy is *not* listening to your soul when it begs you to move. Crazy is worrying that you might look stupid, instead of doing what you want to.

I'm sure there were a lot of people watching her that day who wished they too could be as bold as her. I'm sure there were a lot of people who really wanted to sway their hips and just lose themselves to dance. She was a rule breaker . . . and *you* can be one too.

How do you become comfortable with breaking the rules, and then go ahead and do so? You must first understand that the rules you're governed by are working in a sinister fashion alongside the toxic messages you receive. Living by the 'rules' and toxic messages work side by side

WE COME IN

many

SHAPES,
SIZES,
ETHNICITIES
& ABILITIES.

*Beauty
is diversity.*

EMBRACE YOURSELF

together, plotting a vicious impact on the lives of millions and reigning over everything that we do. If it sounds like I'm describing superhero villains, that's because I am! You are the superhero, and these 'rules' and messages are stripping you of your power!

Let me give you a few examples of how toxic messages and rules work together.

When it comes to ageing, we're often told that looking younger is more beautiful. For example, we see in anti-ageing ads the words 'Defy the lines on your face' or 'Fight the signs of ageing'. The toxic message we receive from this is that only youth is beautiful. The rules we create around ageing then manifest in many ways, such as using phrases like some of these:

'I don't want to look like mutton dressed as lamb.'

'I'm too old to wear that!'

'You should act your age.'

'You are too old to . . .'

When you embrace, like I have, what do you learn to say to those toxic messages and those rules?

You say, 'Wear what you want, when you want.'

How about this example of a toxic message getting into bed with a set of rules? When it comes to beauty, we are told to have smooth, flawless and hairless skin; bright white eyes; a trim, toned waist; perky full breasts; white straight teeth; manicured nails; and beautifully long hair. The rules we create around ageing then manifest in many ways, such as using phrases like some of these:

'My skin is so bad . . .'

'I'm too flat-chested to wear that.'

'You should shave your legs.'

'You can't go out without make-up!'

When you embrace, like I have, what do you learn to say to those toxic messages and those rules?

Beauty is nothing you can see! Beauty is humility, kindness, compassion and humour. We come in many shapes, sizes, ethnicities and abilities. Beauty is diversity!

And of course, there are toxic messages and rules around your weight! When it comes to your weight, you are told that being a certain size will make you happy. Be thin, and conform to a number on the scales. The rules we create around weight then manifest in many ways, such as using phrases like some of these:

'Summer bodies are made in winter.'

'I ate the cake, so now I need to work out . . .'

'People who can't lose weight don't have any self-control.'

'I just need to lose that last five pounds.'

When you embrace, like I have, what do you learn to say to those toxic messages and those rules?

There are no 'bad' foods or 'good' foods – food is just food! Your size and shape don't dictate your health. 'Skinny' people can be unhealthy and 'fat' people can run marathons! Weight does not equal happiness.

EMBRACE YOURSELF

Now that you can unpack the 'rules', and know the toxic messages that helped you build them, it's time to start breaking them! And how do you do that? Ask yourself the following questions:

'What are the rules that have been holding me back?'

'Do these rules serve me and propel me towards the life I want to live?'

'Does living by these rules make me happy?'

'What does life look like when I don't follow the rules?'

Thought-provoking, right? That was only part one! I want you to do *more* than just ponder these questions in your head before putting down this book. I want you to make a commitment to spend some time analysing your rules and asking yourself the questions above, in a space where you can delve deep and reflect. Create a plan, and have a mental vision of what your life will look like when you're a bad-ass rule breaker!

Oh, and just a friendly piece of advice . . . When you start breaking the rules, colouring your hair a different colour and starting your new hip-hop class, be prepared for some resistance from friends and, without a doubt, your family!

Sometimes people struggle with change in their loved ones. It scares them. But just know that as long as you are not hurting anyone, this is *your* life. Live your life *your* way, and as they say all over the internet, 'Buy the shoes, take the trip, eat the cake', and whatever else you please. Above all,

FOLLOW YOUR PASSION AND BREAK FREE OF

your rules to live.

Kenzie Brenna

Body image activist, actor, digital influencer
and founder of Self Love Bootcamp

Breaking rules isn't easy. It's not for the faint of heart. Some of us break them harder than others, but we all benefit from defying convention.

The first rule to break? *Break hate.*

Hatred is easy. We're taught this – we're taught that we aren't enough, that it's more comfortable if everyone just quietly hates themselves at the dinner table. We're taught that it's easier for us to erase ourselves than for us to own our space.

But we have finally caught on. We know that love does not come from a mind that hates.

So, break it. Like I did.

I love my body. Even though I still have low body image days, I fucking love it. I mean *really fucking love it*. It means I love all the stuff I'm supposed to dislike. My curves, my stretchmarks, my skin, my small breasts, my large legs, my scars, my jawline: all of it.

These parts of my body are harmless – beautiful – but they used to hinder me. I used to think of them in a way that held me back from normal human experiences – everything from being social to being able to look into the mirror. Going from execrating my body to embracing it has been one hell of a challenge.

Another rule to break? Love your former self. Yes, the weird, awkward, younger, unlovable you. Love them deeply.

If you time-travelled to your former self – saw yourself struggling, wishing to be a different way, wanting more love than you had – wouldn't you want to hug you? Would you be cruel? Would you shun yourself? Would you silence yourself? Loving your former self breaks down that distance between your past, present and future selves. You are one.

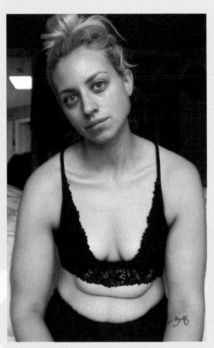 

Your life. Your rules.

You get the chance to say, 'Future me and past me, I love you both.' There is no other feeling like the freedom this brings.

I grew up having an affinity with anger, sadness and anxiousness. My parents got divorced when I was six, my mom had mental health problems of her own, and my dad struggled as well. Stuff that happened in that time defined me.

I realise now that I have a learning disability (although why no tests were done when I was a kid leaves me mystified).

I was always labelled as 'not trying hard enough' or 'not focusing', a story thousands of other people have lived as well. What my parents and teachers also didn't know was that I was a child with panic and stress dysregulation. I was always unusually scared of things happening, and I had sleeping issues as well as eating issues. On top of all this, we moved around quite a bit, so making friends was a struggle.

As I grew older, the panic increased and I began to become more and more disconnected from my body. Hating my body for not looking well, and hating my mind for not working well, started to become the norm.

When I turned thirteen and hit high school, I found rock'n'roll, and I finally had a way of expressing myself. A way to express all those times that I didn't say anything or said too much, was bullied, had fights, cried seemingly for no reason and couldn't explain why, pushed and pulled my parents in every direction. I was finally claiming my voice, but I was doing so through music, drugs, alcohol, self-harm and manipulating my eating patterns.

Want another
rule to smash?
Stop hiding,
stop covering,
stop apologising.

We're taught to seek approval from other people, but only when you start valuing yourself and your own opinion will you stop apologising to those who don't understand you. Only when you start valuing your choices and desires will you stop covering and hiding. Honour yourself so deeply that apologising would be comical.

It wasn't until the last few years when I had some therapy, and started using Instagram to connect and communicate about my problems, that my life started changing. I started to finally see my body as a vessel for experiences instead of something for me to take my anger out on. I have finally been able to find ways to dig deep into my vulnerability, and am at last able to tell my secrets and not feel threatened by them being public. I have embraced everything from wearing T-shirts and tank tops, to having sex with the lights on, to being able to swagger my way through a club. I now feel able to be social and not awkward (mostly), to be content without expectation, and to seize opportunities instead of avoiding them.

You won't think you can do it – you will try to find ways to say that it's too hard or not worth it – but once you start letting go, you'll never look back.It's been a long, hard, worthwhile, wouldn't-trade-it-for-the-world type of journey. Sometimes I still feel like the old me, but that's okay. The old me needs a lot of healing, which may take a lifetime, and that's okay too.

A lifetime spent trying to love feels a lot better than a lifetime spent in hate.

And even if you don't love yourself yet, please know that I do. Know that a whole community of women support you, that we've been there too, and we see and hear you.

Yes, even you.
Especially you.

The last rule to break? *All of these.*
Set your own. Ultimately, it's your life. You have to live by your own boundaries and rules. You have to be your own rule breaker and rule maker. Your life. Your rules.

Weigh it up

TALK A LOT ABOUT CHOICE when it comes to body image. In fact, I've already spoken about choosing happiness earlier in this book! Choice is a funny thing, often causing a divide in the audiences I speak to, as there are passionate arguments on both sides of the debate: whether we are, or are not, in control of our destinies.

Personally I'm a glass-half-full kinda gal, so if you hadn't already guessed, I believe we well and truly have a say in the way our lives pan out. Everything I've done with the Body Image Movement is the result of belief in myself and choosing to believe that what I saw in my head could indeed come to fruition. On the flip side, there are those who believe we've all been dealt certain cards and that, unfortunately, some are lucky enough to have been dealt a queen while others are given a joker.

What puzzles me about those who believe we don't have a choice in life – a choice to rise above the hand we've been dealt – is that idea of acceptance. People who believe their current situation can never change have, I assume, accepted the shitty card they've been dealt as a life sentence. Dealing with that predicament must be pretty tough: constantly wanting what others have, what others are and what others can do. I'm no expert, but it doesn't shock me to hear that rates of depression and anxiety are on the rise worldwide if people are accepting that the way things are now are the way things are always going to be!

The idea of acceptance challenged me beyond belief after I had

my three kids. It's the first time in my life where I felt bound by the hand I'd been dealt. I absolutely hated what my body looked like after having children and could barely look at my reflection in a mirror or window without breaking into tears. I wanted a perfect body like other women had. I wanted to be able to take my kids to the beach and look amazing in a bikini. I wanted to be the mum that others at the school drop-off were in awe of.

When I felt 'stuck' in my body, facing a life sentence of forever hating my body, my acceptance of the situation was missing a key ingredient that I'd called upon for my entire life to help me rise above – choice.

When I was doing dismally at school as a teenager (I still can't believe that same girl has made a documentary and written a book!), I had a choice to stay and accept the unhappiness I was experiencing or to do something differently. Much to the dismay of my mother, I chose the latter and ran away from my Adelaide home (after a short career in washing dishes at my local cafe) to a friend's place in Melbourne.

Did I mention that I was sixteen? I'm not saying it was the best choice –
now that I have kids my heart races just imagining how my mother must
have felt – but the point is that I knew, even as a youngster, that we have
a choice. (*Miki, I'm talking to you now. Don't even THINK about pulling
something like that on me!*)

After accepting that my body was what it was – the result of
carrying, birthing and breastfeeding three kids – and that shedding tears
and feeling hopeless weren't going to change that, I had two options.
I could choose to live within my body and hate it forever, or I could
choose to look for a way to fall in love with it again. Lucky for me,
I chose the latter!

If you've seen *Embrace*, you'll know I explored a number of different
ways to fall in love with the body I was in for the long haul. I went to
a plastic surgeon to explore the idea of transforming my body under the
knife, but that wasn't for me. I took part in a strict regime to transform
my body into that of a fitness model, but that wasn't for me either.
Finally, I chose to stop seeing my body as an ornament and to view it
as the vehicle to my dreams. And you know what? I was finally able to
accept the hand I'd been given. And rather than a cardboard playing card,

I'D BEEN GIFTED A

golden ticket!

Choice. I'm telling you that you have it. No matter how much you
hate your body right now, or how dire your life feels living in it, you too
can choose to love and accept your body.

Pardon the pun, but let's weigh things up!

- Are the ways in which you deal with the body you've got currently serving you?
- What lengths are you willing to go to for the 'perfect body' if you continue refusing to accept your own?
- How long are you willing to sit with body dissatisfaction if you choose not to see things differently?

If this is your 'fork in the road' moment, let me say: you can make a choice as to how you spend the rest of your life. Right here and now.

You have two options. You can choose:

OPTION A (let's call this Option Obey)
Travelling down this road means continuing to hate your body and spending precious time worrying about how it rolls, folds, hangs and sags. The path is frustrating, filled with miserable change-room experiences, embarrassment in the bedroom and fear of going to the beach.

Or, you can choose:

OPTION B (or, as I like to say, Option Yay!)
Walking, skipping, jumping or sashaying down this road of unconditional love for your body means respecting yourself, keeping the lights on when you ride your partner like you're at a rodeo in your very own bedroom, and doing giant, joyful bombs into the pool.

'If only it were that simple,' I hear you say. Well, it is. Making the choice to embrace is your first step. It's just the beginning. I never said anything about flicking a switch and having immediate and unwavering body acceptance once you've chosen which road you'll travel.

By now you know that this is going to be a process, and there will be days that are sublime and some that (let's be frank) are utter shit. There will be days when you need to push through, faking it until you make it. But no matter what your day looks like, you are the best version of you when you choose a life filled with 'yay' over pointless hours conforming to 'obey'.

Someone I met during this body-loving journey, whom I now consider a dear friend, recently shared with me one of the ways she was able to accept her body and then choose to embrace it. It sounded a little ridiculous at first, but the more I think about it, the more I think her idea is ingenious.

She had a funeral for her former self.

Accepting your body and choosing the path to embrace it requires you to also accept that you are never going to treat yourself or your body the way you once did. You are saying goodbye to a former part of yourself, the part that used to hate your body, criticise your body and try to manipulate your body and its set weight point. Saying goodbye to who you formerly were can fill you with immense grief, and that part of yourself deserves to be honoured. Yes, as a body loather you were miserable and unhappy, but that former part of yourself also served to protect you (albeit unnecessarily). Your former self that stayed inside on sunny days to prevent your body from being on show was trying to save you the embarrassment. The former part of yourself that exercised relentlessly to lose weight was trying to give you the body you thought you needed. Your old self deserves a goodbye, and what better way than with a funeral.

I'm not suggesting you hire a hall and share your new path to body love with your nearest and dearest. I'm suggesting that you need to make peace with moving on, as my friend did. She packed a bag with all the 'skinny' clothes she kept in her wardrobe, waiting to one day fit back into, and drove it to her local charity shop. She then deleted her calorie

counting apps, the alarms that woke her to exercise each morning and a folder of photos she referenced daily for inspiration of her former self looking thinner. Sitting in her car, she sobbed as she realised that part of herself was no longer with her, that it was gone. She told me she cried remembering the pain of always feeling ugly, how good she felt when someone told her she looked thinner, the wasted hours she spent weighing food, and the countless occasions in life she missed out on. She also cried in fear of what her new existence would look like, a life without actively manipulating her body.

However, when the tears dried, much like a send-off or farewell, she was filled with peace and hope for what the next day would bring.

Acceptance can be hard, but the body you have is the *only* one you're going to be given. The brilliant part is that you now have a choice: a choice to continue living a life sentence in a body you hate, or to experience the freedom and joy that comes with embracing.

In your decision-making process, I want you to keep this in mind: every breath you take is one step closer to your last, so don't delay. If you're lucky enough to live until you're eighty, you have around 29 000 days from birth to death to experience all life has to give.

Doesn't sound like much, does it? It isn't! How many days have you lived so far? And how many days might you have until the end? And the most important question of them all: how are you going to fill those days? I hope, for your sake, that you fill them with unconditional love for your body because that's what you deserve.

CAN YOU HEAR ME? YOUR BODY
deserves your love.

At the beginning of this book, I questioned whether my words on paper would be as profound and powerful as the effect I can have on an auditorium's audience. I'm no longer questioning myself and whether my message can get across to you. That uncertainty is now gone – I'm that much more confident in this moment than I have ever been on stage. Tears are rolling down my face, because I am here, with you. I've felt your pain, and now I feel your optimism.

So go forth, friend and embrace.

BECAUSE YOUR BODY
IS NOT AN ORNAMENT.
It is the vehicle to your dreams.

Taryn xox

WEIGH IT UP

EMBRACE YOURSELF

References

What I Want for You

'This was the most common regret of all . . .' See Bronnie Ware, *The Top Five Regrets of the Dying* (Hay House) 2012.

The Current State of Play

'In 2015, a study by the International Society of Aesthetic Plastic Surgery . . .' See https://www.isaps.org/wp-content/uploads/2017/10/2016-ISAPS-Results-1.pdf.

Fuck Off!

'The estimated number of commercials the average American girl has seen . . .' See *Miss Representation* documentary, directed and produced by Jennifer Siebel Newsom, Ro*co Films Educational 2011.

'Candidly, we go after the cool kids . . .' See Benoit Denizet-Lewis, 'The Man Behind Abercrombie & Fitch,' 24 January 2006, www.salon.com/2006/01/24/jeffries.

'A 2012 study by scientific journal PLOS ONE noted that there seemed to be a discrepancy . . .' See Lynda G. Boothroyd, Martin J. Tovée, Thomas V. Pollet, 'Visual Diet Versus Associative Learning as Mechanisms of Change in Body Size Preferences,' *PLOS ONE*, 7 November 2012.

The Highlight Reel Ain't Real

'According to Jennifer Berger, Executive Director of About-Face, a staggering 95 per cent of the . . .' See https://www.traffika.com.au/blog/7-ways-photoshop-changed-world-infographic/.

'Scarier still is research conducted by Dr Marilyn Bromberg, Senior Lecturer in Law at the University of Western Australia. She has found that everyday women . . .' See Bromberg, M., Halliwell, C. 2017, '"All About That Bass" and Photoshopping a Model's Waist: Introducing Body Image Law', *University of Notre Dame Australia Law Review*, 18, pp. 1–19.

REFERENCES

CONTRIBUTOR PHOTO CREDITS

PAGE VIII: photograph by Teresa's friend Jessica Bolt

PAGE 18: photographs provided by Jane Gardiner

PAGE 41: photograph by Sovereign Grace Howie

PAGE 79: photograph (left) provided by Jes Baker, (right) by Jessy Parr

PAGE 115: photograph by Jade Beall

PAGES 126, 129: photographs by Tarryn Rudolph

PAGE 137: photograph by Megan Jayne Crabbe

PAGE 138: photograph by Deborah Svoboda

PAGE 148: photograph by Maria Porter

PAGE 149: photograph by Joel Blakeley

PAGE 171: photographs by Kenzie Brenna

HEY YOU ...
WANT TO HANG OUT SOME MORE?

EMBRACE *you*

Join me and the thousands of women around the world who are supercharging their journey to embrace with my 4-week online program Embrace You.

start today

- Reignite your mojo and passion for life
- Full of life-changing practical strategies
- 4 weekly videos from me and my experts
- Free workbook full of inspiration
- 12 months of ongoing support
- Lifetime access to all resources

embraceyouonline.com

Contributors

Dr Linda Bacon
lindabacon.org

Jes Baker
themilitantbaker.com

Celeste Barber
celestebarber.com

Jade Beall
jadebeall.com

Kenzie Brenna
kenziebrenna.com

Megan Jayne Crabbe
bodyposipanda.com

Jane Gardiner
bodyimagemovement.com/bimgas/
jane-gardiner/

Louise Green
louisegreen.ca

Amy D. Herrmann
underneathiam.com

Nigel Marsh
nigelmarsh.com

Jess Smith
jessicasmith.com.au

Acknowledgements

I'M PARALYSED WITH FEAR WRITING THIS LIST OF ACKNOWLEDGEMENTS because I'm petrified of leaving someone off the list! So, if you think you should be here and you're not, I'm really sorry. Take me off your Christmas card list – there, we're even!

First, to the delightful Ali Watts and the team at Penguin Random House Australia. Thank you for your vision in seeing this book come to life, and giving me the confidence to believe I could write it. Ali, you are such a pleasure to work with. Thanks for championing this book; it exists because of you.

To Michaela Skilney, my friendly Pai Mei and loving wing-woman. Thank you for helping me stay on track and for being an effervescent energy of pure delight. You took my words and shaped them into a structure that flowed and made sense, and I will be forever grateful.

Thank you Teresa Palmer for your beautiful foreword. It's a pleasure standing alongside you, advocating for positive body image. The fact that you are from Radelaide makes you even more awesome!

Thank you to my global sisters and contributors in this book: Jane Gardiner, Celeste Barber, Amy D. Herrmann, Jes Baker, Nigel Marsh (hmm hmm 'uncle'), Jade Beall, Louise Green, Megan Jayne Crabbe, Dr Linda Bacon, Jess Smith and Kenzie Brenna. I've shared real-life hugs with you all, I've looked into your eyes, I've seen your souls. I love who you are, what you do and how you make the world a better place.

Thank you to my loyal dream team at the Body Image Movement –
Prue Langhans, Tamara Doig, Josephine Ainscough, Kate Burr and
all of the Body Image Movement Global Ambassadors (BIMGAs).
Honestly, lovelies, you keep me fed, caffeinated, loved and supported,
and I am so grateful to work alongside you every day.

Big hugs and thanks to my favourite photographer Meg Hansen –
the images in this book simply rock! You are a dream to work with.
Thanks for the laughs and all of your hard work. Thanks to other
photography contributions from Prue Langhans, Kate Ellis,
Karen Lynch, Benjamin Liew, Katherine Schultz and Andre Agnew.

Thanks also to Bettyanne and Geoffrey (the parentals), Justine
and the Bransons, Jason Butterworth, Ceinwen Ahern, Daria Yeatman,
Nora Tschirner, Emma Isaacs, Mia Freedman, Dr Emma Johnston, Lorna
Jane Clarkson, Olivia Newton-John, Georgie Gardner, Ricki Lake, Akira
Chan, Renee Airya, Joe Polish, Turia Pitt, Ellen DeGeneres, Harnaam
Kaur, Dr Marilyn Bromberg, Stefania Ferrario, Tenisha Ortiz, Ellen
Briggs, Paul Ward, Blanca Lista, Benjamin Speed, Amanda Nash, Andrea
Hall, Anna Vincent, Tim White, Bettina Hamilton, Lindi Harrison, Bryan
Mason, Bonnie McBride, the *Embrace* documentary production team,
the 8909 Kickstarter backers, Christine and Adam for your gorgeous
1950s kitchen, Norwood Swimming centre, Harvey the label, Revive
Fitness Centre, Sally from Mojoco, Blue Scarab and the delightful
Jane Cay and all the birds at birdsnest.

And finally, the most important people in my life: Mathew, Oliver,
Cruz, Mikaela and Chico. (While Chico's not a human, he sure is treated
like one!) Thank you, my loves. You are my rocks, my life, my everything.
I'm grateful every day to share this experience with you all and I couldn't
do what I do without your unconditional love and support. I love you
more than chocolate.

ACKNOWLEDGEMENTS